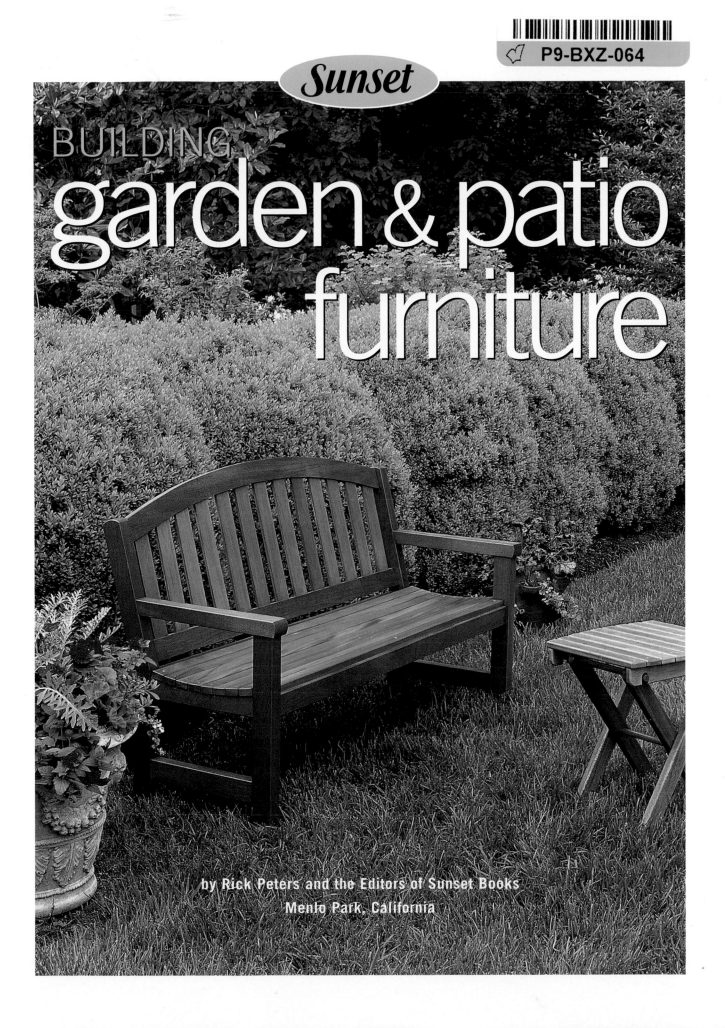

Sunset

BUILDING
garden & patio furniture

by Rick Peters and the Editors of Sunset Books
Menlo Park, California

about this book

Building Garden & Patio Furniture features 18 woodworking projects that suit skills from beginner to advanced. Some can be built easily in an afternoon, while others require more time and advanced construction techniques. Once you've found the projects you want to make in Chapter 1, don't forget to check out Chapter 2 for basics on materials, tools, assembly techniques, and finishes before you begin.

SAFETY Woodworking is inherently dangerous. Care must be taken when using hand and power tools to prevent injury. Take proper safety precautions including wearing eye protection, donning a respirator to protect your lungs, and always use the guards that come with power tools (note:

guards have been removed in some step-by-step photos for clarity). Don't perform operations shown in this book unless you're certain they are safe for you. If something doesn't feel safe, don't do it. Look for an alternative method. Keep safety foremost in your mind while working in the shop.

ACKNOWLEDGEMENTS We would like to thank the following designers and homeowners for allowing us to photograph our projects at their homes: Yunghi Choi, Landscape Architect, Washington DC; Tom Mannion Landscape Design, Arlington, VA; Sam Williamson, Portland, OR; James and Donna Hackman; Susan Klee and Eric Cummings; and Caroline McCumber. Thanks also to Will Doyle, Veer Newaldass, and Johnny Gay for their valuable assistance.

SUNSET BOOKS

Vice President & General Manager: Richard A. Smeby
Vice President & Editorial Director: Bob Doyle
Production Director: Lory Day
Director of Operations: Rosann Sutherland
Sales Development Director: Linda Barker

STAFF FOR THIS BOOK

Managing Editor: Bridget Biscotti Bradley
Furniture Design and Text: Rick Peters
Art Director: Vasken Guiragossian
Principal Photographer: Christopher Vendetta
Illustrator: Jerry O'Brien
Photo Stylist: Jane Martin
Page Production: Janie Farn
Copyeditor: Barbara McIntosh Webb
Proofreader: Audrey Mak
Production Coordinator: Eligio Hernandez
Indexer: Nanette Cardon

Additional photography credits:
Roger Foley: cover, 1, 3 top, 4, 10, 14, 20, 24, 30, 38, 44, 50, 56, 62, 68, 72, 78, 84, 88, 94, 104; Thomas J. Story: 100.

10 9 8 7 6 5 4 3 2 1

First printing October 2002

Library of Congress Catalog Card Number: 2002108856.
ISBN 0-376-01027-4
Printed in the United States.

For additional copies of *Building Garden & Patio Furniture* or any other Sunset book, call 1-800-526-5111 or visit us at www.sunset.com.

Projects

Materials, Tools, and Techniques

adirondack chair

Easy to make, easy to look at, and easy to enjoy anywhere. Just cut out the parts, then bolt and screw the pieces together—that's how simple it is to make this classic, enduring chair.

- **Material:** Pine
- **Adhesive:** Titebond II
- **Finish:** 1 coat oil-based primer; 2 coats white satin enamel
- **Level:** Easy

PATTERNS

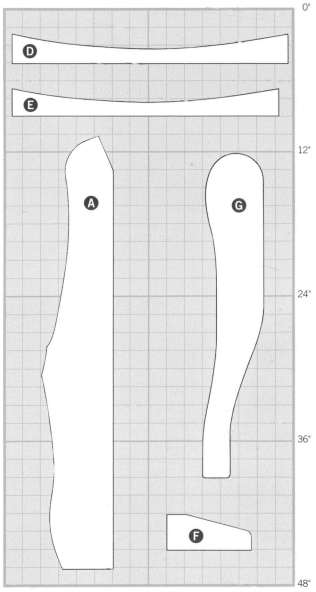

One square = 1½"

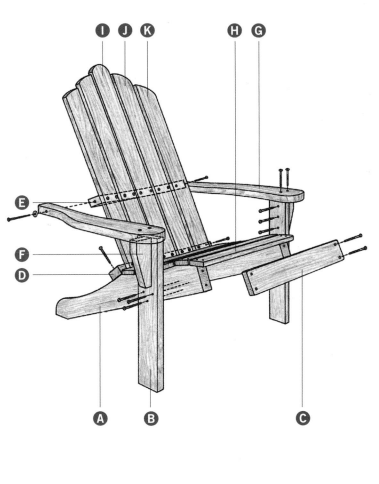

This namesake of New York's Adirondack Mountains was originally called something else: the Westport chair, after a town on Lake Champlain. Thomas Lee, vacationing at his Westport summer home in the early 1900s, wanted a comfortable outdoor chair. After experimenting with pine planks, he produced the sloping angles and wide armrests that are the hallmark of the Adirondack style. Build this classic and the matching patio table on page 68.

MATERIALS LIST

PART	NAME	QUANTITY	DIMENSIONS
A	Rear legs	2	6" × 36" – 1½" stock
B	Front legs	2	3½" × 22" – ¾" stock
C	Front rail	1	4" × 23" – ¾" stock
D	Lower back support	1	2½" × 23" – 1½" stock
E	Upper back support	1	2½" × 22¼" – 1½" stock
F	Arm supports	2	3" × 7" – 1½" stock
G	Arms	2	5" × 27" – 1½" stock
H	Seat slats	6	2½" × 24" – ¾" stock
I	Center back slat	1	4" × 38" – ¾" stock
J	Middle back slats	2	4" × 36" – ¾" stock
K	End back slats	2	4" × 33½" – ¾" stock

Assembly Instructions

The Adirondack chair consists of two sides connected by a front rail and two back supports. The seat and back are made up of separate slats that are screwed to the sides and back supports (see the illustration on page 5). To begin construction, start by cutting the pieces to length and width according to the materials list. Then, make full-sized patterns for the rear leg, arm, arm support, and back supports from the scale drawings on page 5.

1 Once the parts are cut to size and the patterns made, the first step is to transfer the rear leg pattern to the two rear leg blanks (A). A blank is a piece that's cut to rough size and is ready to be shaped. Place the pattern on each blank and trace around it with a pencil.

2 Now you can cut the rear legs to shape. A saber saw works fine for this, but a band saw will make quicker work of the job. When you're done sawing the legs to shape, sand the rough edges smooth with a drum sander in a drill press or in a portable electric drill. Next, rout a ⅜-inch round-over on all edges of the rear legs and a ¼-inch round-over on the front edges of the front legs (but not the top edge).

3 To assemble the sides, attach the rear legs (A) to the front legs (B). Since there's a right and a left side assembly, it's important to create a book-matched pair. Temporarily clamp a front leg to a rear leg, making sure the bottom of the front leg is flat and the rear leg protrudes past the front leg as shown in step 4. At the same time, use a try square to make sure the front leg is plumb. When everything is correct, secure the front leg to the rear leg with three #8 × 2-inch woodscrews.

4 To connect the sides, start by routing a ¼-inch round-over on the front rail (C). Then hold it in place on the ends of each of the rear legs so the edges are flush, and drill countersunk pilot holes. Attach the front rail with 3-inch galvanized deck screws.

5 The back ends of the sides are connected with the lower back support (D). Start by transferring the back support pattern to the blank and cut it to shape. Mark and cut the upper back support (E) at the same time. Sand the curves on both of these smooth and then rout a ¼-inch round-over on the back edges only. The lower back support is attached to the rear leg at the small flats; place the support on the flats and drill ⁹⁄₃₂-inch pilot holes through the support and into the leg. Then secure the support to the legs with ⁵⁄₁₆-inch × 5-inch lag screws.

6 With the sides connected, the next step is to attach the seat slats. You'll need to shorten two of the six seat slats to fit between the front legs; leave the others a full 24 inches. Before attaching them, rout a ¼-inch round-over on the top long edges only of each slat. Let the front slat extend ½ inch past the front rail, and then attach the remaining slats using ³⁄₈-inch spacers between the slats. Make sure the ends of each slat extend an equal amount past the sides and then drill countersunk pilot holes and secure them with #8 × 2-inch screws.

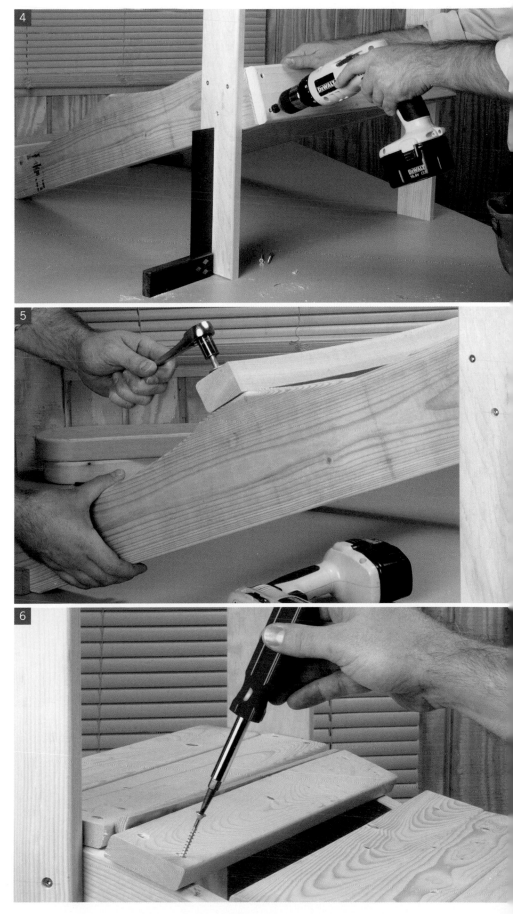

7 With the seat assembled, you can turn your attention to the arms. Start by transferring the arm support pattern to the arm support blanks (F). Cut them to shape and sand the edges smooth. Then rout a ¼-inch round-over on the front edges only. Temporarily clamp an arm support to the front leg so it's centered on its width and flush at the top. Then drill countersunk pilot holes and attach the arm support to the front leg with #8 × 2-inch screws.

8 Now transfer the arm patterns to the arm blanks (G); keep in mind you're making a matched pair here. Then cut the arms to shape and sand the rough edges smooth. Next, lay out and drill a ⁵⁄₁₆-inch shank hole in the narrow end of each arm for the lag screws; these holes are centered on the thickness of the stock and are 2½ inches in from the ends. The last step before attaching the arms is to rout a ³⁄₈-inch round-over on all edges. Now working on one arm at a time, position the arm so it extends past the front leg 1½ inches in front and ½ inch on the sides. To hold the arm in place, temporarily clamp a scrap to the inside of each rear leg to support the arms; make sure the arms are level and clamp the back edge to the scrap. Then drill countersunk pilot holes and secure the arms to the arm supports with 3-inch deck screws.

9 To connect the back ends of the arms, position the upper back support between the arms and drill ⁹⁄₃₂-inch pilot holes through the arms and into the upper back support. Attach upper back support to the arms with ⁵⁄₁₆-inch × 5-inch lag screws.

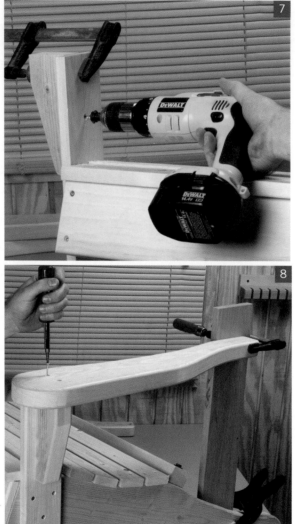

10 All that's left to complete the chair is to add the back slats. Start by laying out the curve on the top of each slat; use the patterns shown on page 69. Once you've laid out the curves, cut them to shape and sand the ends smooth. Then rout a ¼-inch round-over on all the edges but

the bottom ends. To position the slats, first locate and mark the center points on the lower and upper back supports; also, mark the center points of the center back slat (I). Align the marks on the center slat with the marks you made on the back supports, and temporarily clamp the center back slat in place. Use a try square to make sure the slat is plumb to the back supports.

11 Now drill a pair of countersunk pilot holes through the center slat and into the upper support and secure it with #8 × 2-inch screws. Repeat this at the bottom of the slat.

12 With the center slat secured, position the middle and end slats (J, K) and arrange them for an even gap between the slats. Here again, temporarily clamp each slat in place, drill pairs of countersunk pilot holes through the slats and into the supports, and secure each slat with screws.

13 Sand the entire chair with 150-grit sandpaper. If you've used a hardwood such as white oak and want a clear finish, apply a couple of coats of satin spar varnish, sanding between coats. For the painted look, apply a coat of oil-based primer followed by two coats of satin enamel; sand between coats.

collapsible chair

Without a single hinge or piece of hardware, this extremely comfortable chair pulls apart to collapse for storage in small spaces. The secret? Interlocking cleats. Caution: Make one, and you'll be asked for several more.

- **Material:** Mahogany
- **Adhesive:** None
- **Finish:** None
- **Level:** Easy

PATTERNS

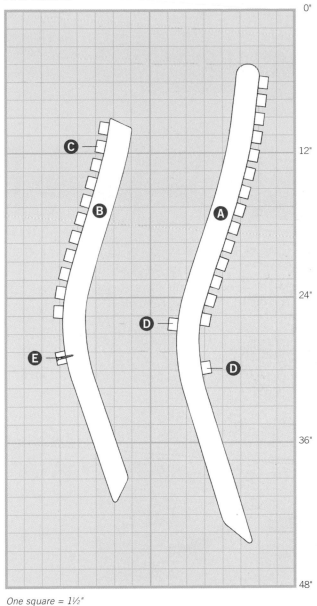

One square = 1½"

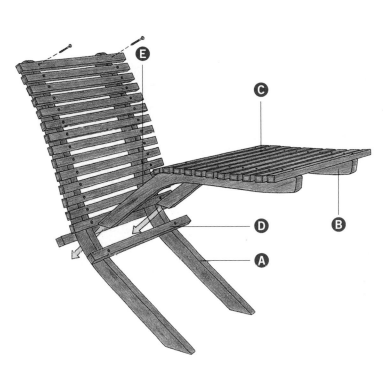

Family, friends, random passers-by—everyone will want one of these great all-around collapsible chairs. When you need it, it's surprisingly supportive; when you don't, the two components pull apart and nestle together for compact storage. It's quick and easy: Cut a couple of curved legs and then screw on the slats. We left this chair unfinished so that it can slowly age to a lovely, weathered gray.

MATERIALS LIST

PART	NAME	QUANTITY	DIMENSIONS
A	Back legs	2	2" × 40" – ⁵/₄ stock
B	Front legs	2	2" × 32" – ⁵/₄ stock
C	Slats	25	1" × 20" – ³/₄" stock
D	Front cleats	2	1" × 20" – ³/₄" stock
E	Back cleat	1	1" × 13" – ³/₄" stock

Assembly Instructions

The collapsible chair consists of two separate units: the back and front legs, and the seat and back legs (see the illustration on page 11). The seat and back are simply slats that are screwed to the legs. To begin construction, cut the parts to width and length according to the materials list. Then make full-sized patterns of the front and back legs from the scale drawings on page 11.

1 Transfer the back leg pattern onto the wood; if you nestle two together, you can get them both out of a single 9-inch-wide blank. Then cut the back legs (A) to rough shape.

2 The next step is to sand the legs smooth. Fasten them together with double-sided tape so you can sand them at the same time and they'll come out a perfect match. When you're done with the back legs, cut the front legs (B) to shape and sand the edges smooth.

3 With the legs done, start work on the slats (C). Begin by sanding a chamfer on the ends. Although you can do this by hand, it's tedious and the chamfer will

not be uniform. A simple way to create a uniform chamfer is to clamp a pair of 45-degree scraps to the table of a disk sander. The left scrap guides the slat in at the correct angle; the right scrap serves as a stop to halt sanding once a 1/8-inch chamfer is created. Push a slat forward until it hits the right scrap, then pull it back, rotate the slat, and push forward again; repeat for the remaining edges.

4 To complete the slats, drill countersunk shank holes for screws centered on each of the 14 back slats, 3 inches in from the ends. Drill holes 4 1/8 inches in from the ends on the 11 seat slats. Then soften all the edges with sandpaper.

5 Assemble the halves of the chair by first cutting two 13-inch-wide spacers for the front legs. Then clamp these between the legs, making sure the ends of the legs are flush. Position the first slat so it extends equally on both sides and so it's 3/4 inch down from the top of the leg. Drill pilot holes through the slat and into the legs and secure it with #8 × 2-inch screws. Attach the remaining back slats using a 1/2-inch spacer between each slat.

6 The back leg/seat unit is assembled just like the front leg/back unit, except the spacers are only 10¾ inches long. Also, to soften the front edge of the seat, rout a ¼-inch round-over on one slat. This first slat is set back ¼ inch from the front of the unit. Use spacers and work toward the rear, attaching slats. Here again, position the slats so they extend an equal amount on each side.

7 Now add the cleats that lock the two units together. Slip the two halves of the chair together and apply clamps to hold it upright; keep the leg bottoms flat on the work surface. Then drill countersunk pilot holes and attach both front cleats (D) to the front leg/back unit as shown. Finally, drill countersunk pilot holes and attach the back cleat to the seat/front leg unit as shown. Sand all parts with 150-grit sandpaper, and apply the finish of your choice.

dining chair

Strong, sturdy, and straightforward: This is a dining chair to relax and linger in. Designed to accommodate an ample seat, its clean lines and simple production techniques make this one easy to build in quantity.

- **Material:** White oak
- **Adhesive:** Titebond II
- **Finish:** 2 coats of satin spar varnish
- **Level:** Moderate

PATTERNS

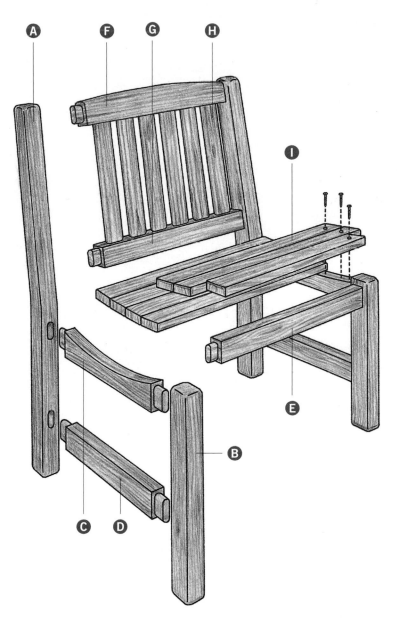

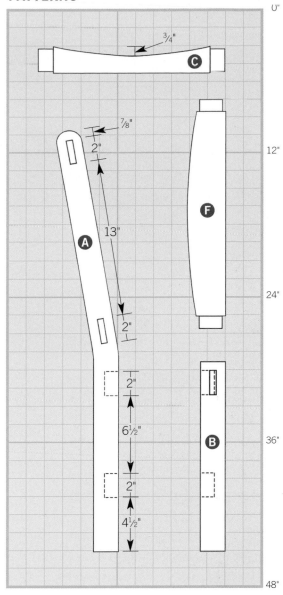

One square = 1½"

S tout joinery shapes rugged white oak into an unusually roomy chair that looks as distinctive as it is. Cushions? Not here. An extra few inches of width, plus the slightly curved, dished seat, demonstrate how comfortable a "hard" wooden chair can be. For a truly custom patio set, make four or more to accompany the tile dining table on page 88.

MATERIALS LIST

PART	NAME	QUANTITY	DIMENSIONS
A	Back legs	2	2" × 35" – ⁸/4 stock
B	Front legs	2	2" × 15³/4" – ⁸/4 stock
C	Seat rails	2	2¹/4" × 15¹/2" – 1³/8" stock
D	Bottom rails	2	2¹/4" × 15¹/2" – 1³/8" stock
E	Front rail	1	2¹/4" × 19¹/8" – ⁵/4 stock
F	Back top	1	3¹/4" × 19¹/8" – ⁵/4 stock
G	Back bottom	1	2¹/2" × 19¹/8" – ⁵/4 stock
H	Back slats	6	1⁷/8" × 13⁵/8" – ¹/2" stock
I	Seat slats	7	2" × 20⁵/8" – ³/4" stock

Assembly Instructions

The dining chair is made up of two side assemblies joined with a front rail and a back top and bottom (see the illustration on page 15). The back top and bottom hold a set of slats that forms the back. Each side assembly consists of a front and back leg joined by a seat and bottom rail. Slats are screwed to the curved seat rails to create a comfortable seat. To start, cut the parts to width and length according to the materials list. Then create full-sized patterns for the front and back leg, using the scale drawings on page 15.

1 Begin work on the side assemblies by transferring the pattern of the back leg to a blank; you can get two legs from a blank that's $6\frac{3}{4}$ inches × 40 inches. Cut the back legs (A) to rough shape on the band saw or with a saber saw. Then smooth the faces with a hand plane and sand the rounded ends.

2 Next, lay out the mortise locations on the back (A) and front (B) legs using the template, taking care to make book-matched sets.

3 Now use the mortising jig shown on page 122 to rout the mortises in the legs. The seat and bottom rail mortises are $\frac{3}{4}$ inch

wide and $1\frac{1}{4}$ inches deep; the back and top bottom mortises are $\frac{1}{2}$ inch wide and 1 inch deep. The mortising jig can't handle mortises for the back top, as they're too near the end. Instead, drill out the waste and chisel the sides smooth. Once you've cut the mortises, rout a $\frac{1}{4}$ inch round-over on all edges of the front and back legs.

5 Next lay out the gentle curve on the top edge of the seat rails. Clamp a thin strip of wood to the ends of the rail so the center of the curve is ¾ inch down from the top edge (or make a template from ¼-inch hardboard). Trace around the curve with a pencil. Then cut the curve to shape on the band saw or with a saber saw and sand the edges smooth.

4 To join the legs together, cut 1¼-inch-long tenons on the ends of the seat (C) and bottom (D) rails to fit the mortises in the legs. Use the miter gauge to guide the rail and set the rip fence to define the shoulders of the tenon. Then round over the corners of the tenons with a 4-in-1 rasp or square up the mortises with a sharp chisel.

6 Now you can assemble the sides. Start by dry-fitting all the parts with clamps to check the fit. If everything goes together well, spread glue on the tenons of the seat and bottom rails and slide these into the front and back legs. Apply clamps and allow the sides to dry overnight.

7 With the sides complete, you can begin work on the front rail (E) and the back top and bottom (F, G). Start by cutting ½-inch-wide, 1-inch-long tenons on the ends to fit the mortises in the back legs. Use the miter gauge to guide the workpiece and set the rip fence to define the shoulders of the tenons.

8 The back slats (H) fit into matching mortises routed in the back top and bottom. If you're building a set of chairs, consider making a jig to speed up the work (see opposite page). Use the mortising jig to rout ½-inch-deep mortises for the back slats in the back top and bottom. Then rout a ¼-inch round-over on the long edges of the back slats (H) so they'll fit in the round mortises.

9 With the mortise cut, the next step is to lay out the top arch on the back top (F). The curve starts 2½ inches up from the bottom edge at each end and is centered on the width of the back top. Clamp a thin strip of wood to the top; or better yet, make a template from ¼-inch hardboard and trace around it. Cut the top curve to shape on the band saw or with a saber saw, and sand the edges smooth. Because of this curved cut, you'll need to trim the tops of the tenons to fit into the mortises in the rear leg.

10 Start final assembly by gluing the back slats into the back top and bottom. Then apply glue to the tenons of the back top and bottom and the front rail, and assemble the chair with clamps.

11 Finally, round over all edges of the seat slats (I) with a ¼-inch round-over bit. Then lay out and drill countersunk pilot holes to attach the slats; these holes are centered on the width of the slats and are ⅞ inch in from the ends. Position the seat rails on the seat with even gaps between them, and drill pilot holes for #8 × 1½-inch screws. Then screw the slats to the seat rails. Note: You'll need to trim the front seat slat to fit between the front legs before attaching it to the front rail (E).

Routing Multiple Mortises

When faced with routing multiple mortises in a group of similar parts (like the back top and bottom for a set of chairs), it's well worth the time and effort to make a custom jig. The routing jig shown here uses a ⅝-inch guide bushing in the router. The jig is just a piece of ¼-inch hardboard with ⅝-inch-wide mortises accurately cut into it. Use a Forstner bit on the drill press with a fence to make these, by drilling a series of overlapping holes.

Attach the template to a pair of side cleats to grip the workpiece (depending on how tight this fit is, you may or may not need clamps to hold the workpiece in place). Slide a back top or bottom into the jig so the ends are flush, and clamp it in a vise. Then, using a plunge router fitted with a ½-inch straight bit, set the bushing in one of the holes in the template and cut the mortise. Repeat for the remaining mortises.

simple bench

Form and function blend in this easy-to-make accent or dining piece. It uses "honest" joinery—a tusked mortise-and-tenon joint. The tusk not only reinforces the joint but also serves as a decorative element.

- **Material:** Cedar
- **Adhesive:** Titebond II
- **Finish:** 2 coats of satin spar varnish
- **Level:** Easy

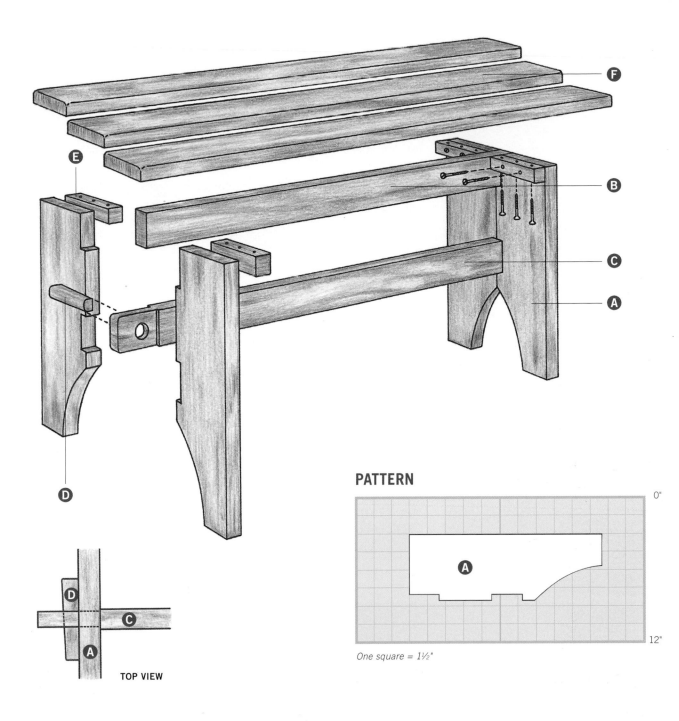

PATTERN

0"

Ⓐ

12"

One square = 1½"

TOP VIEW

You don't need a lot of time or high-end experience to craft this appealing bench. It's an afternoon project that will have you sitting in the garden in no time. As a stand-alone piece, this one works great, but its versatility doesn't stop there. Consider using it with a dining table—like the folding version on page 78 or the round table shown on page 72.

MATERIALS LIST

PART	NAME	QUANTITY	DIMENSIONS
A	Leg sections	4	5½" × 16" – 1" stock
B	Top stretcher	1	2½" × 30" – 1" stock
C	Bottom stretcher	1	2½" × 34" – 1" stock
D	Tusks	2	1" × 4" – 1" stock
E	Seat cleats	4	1¼" × 5" – 1" stock
F	Seat slats	3	4½" × 37½" – 1" stock

Assembly Instructions

The simple bench is made up of two legs connected with a pair of stretchers and the top. The top is made up of three separate slats and is secured to the sides with cleats (see the top illustration on page 21). To start construction, cut the parts to length and width per the materials list, and make a full-sized pattern for leg sections from the scale drawing on page 21.

1 Each leg has two sections (A). The advantage to this is that you can create mortises for the stretchers by cutting notches in each section and then joining them together. Begin by transferring the leg section pattern to the four leg sections. Position the pattern on the piece and trace around it. Since you'll be making book-matched pairs, take the time to select the best grain and label the parts as pairs.

2 The next step is to cut notches to create the mortises for the stretchers. These are ⅜ inch deep in each section to form ¾-inch-wide mortises. The simplest way to cut these is with a dado blade on the table saw. Attach an auxiliary fence to the miter gauge for better support, and use the rip fence as a stop to define the ends of the cuts. Then cut out the curve with a saber saw or band saw and sand the edges smooth.

3 To strengthen the joint between the leg sections, cut slots in the mating edges for biscuits with a biscuit joiner or drill holes for dowels. Then apply glue and biscuits or dowels, and glue the leg sections together.

4 The legs are connected together with the top and bottom stretchers (B, C). The shorter top stretcher fits between the legs; the longer bottom stretcher extends out past the legs and has a hole in it to accept the tusks that pull the mortise-and-tenon joint together. Cut a 1-inch-long, ¾-inch-wide tenon on both ends of the top stretcher, and a 3¾-inch-long, ¾-inch-wide tenon on both ends of the top stretcher. Sand, file, or plane a ¼-inch chamfer on the ends of the long tenon.

5 Next, drill a 1-inch-diameter hole centered on the width of the bottom stretcher 1¾ inches in from each end to accept the tusks. Then sand, chisel, or file a gentle taper on one end of each tusk (D). The idea here is to pull the joint tight when the tusk is roughly centered in the tenon.

6 To assemble the bench, start by gluing the stretchers into the mortises in the legs, and drive a tusk through the hole in each bottom stretcher. Then drill counterbored shank holes through the seat cleats (E) for the screws that will hold the seat slats in place. Glue and screw the seat cleats to the tops of the legs, taking care to make sure the top edges are flush.

7 Lay the seat slats (F) face down on a table. Insert ¼-inch spacers between the slats, and clamp the slats together temporarily. Center the assembled base upside down on the slats from end to end and from side to side. Then drive screws through the cleats and into the seat slats. Sand the bench with 150-grit sandpaper and apply the finish of your choice.

classic bench

Great lines, a graceful arch, and simple, timeless design…it's tough to beat this beautiful yet sturdy addition to any yard, deck, or patio. A match for advanced skills, this project will reward you for years to come.

- **Material:** Mahogany
- **Adhesive:** Resorcinol
- **Finish:** 2 coats of satin exterior polyurethane
- **Level:** Challenging

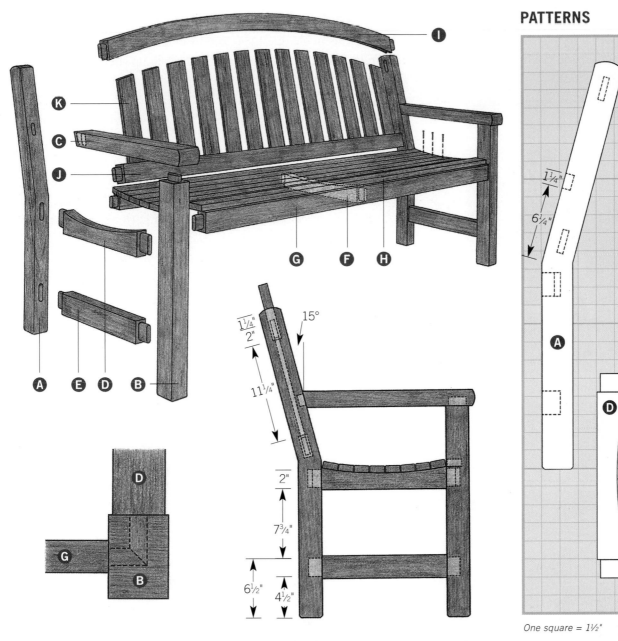

PATTERNS

0"

$1\frac{1}{4}$"

$6\frac{1}{4}$"

12"

A

24"

D

$\frac{3}{4}$"

36"

48"

One square = 1½"

$\frac{1\frac{1}{4}"}{2"}$

15°

$11\frac{1}{4}$"

2"

$7\frac{3}{4}$"

$6\frac{1}{2}$" $4\frac{1}{2}$"

MATERIALS LIST

PART	NAME	QUANTITY	DIMENSIONS
A	Rear legs	2	$2\frac{1}{2}$" × 34" – $1\frac{3}{4}$" stock
B	Front legs	2	$2\frac{1}{2}$" × $24\frac{1}{4}$" – $1\frac{3}{4}$" stock
C	Arms	2	$2\frac{1}{2}$" × 20" – $1\frac{3}{4}$" stock
D	Seat supports	2	$2\frac{1}{2}$" × 17" – $1\frac{1}{2}$" stock
E	Bottom rails	2	$2\frac{1}{2}$" × 17" – $1\frac{1}{2}$" stock
F	Middle seat support	1	$2\frac{1}{2}$" × $17\frac{1}{2}$" – $1\frac{3}{4}$" stock
G	Front/back stretchers	2	$2\frac{1}{2}$" × $57\frac{3}{4}$" – $1\frac{3}{4}$" stock
H	Seat slats	9	$1\frac{5}{8}$" × $59\frac{1}{4}$" – $\frac{3}{4}$" stock
I	Back top	1	7" × $57\frac{3}{4}$" – 1" stock
J	Back bottom	1	$2\frac{1}{2}$" × $57\frac{3}{4}$" – 1" stock
K	Back slats	13	$2\frac{1}{2}$" × $16\frac{1}{2}$"* – $\frac{3}{8}$" stock

*rough length (see illustration on page 29)

Like many things we call classic, this bench is simple—but not easy. At nearly 5 feet long, it offers ample seating in a style that will blend well with just about any environment. The faux mortises on the back slats make construction simple, but don't be deceived: You won't whip this one together in an afternoon. You will be glad, though, that you took your time.

Assembly Instructions

The classic bench is made up of two side assemblies connected with stretchers, and a back top and bottom. Slats make up the seat and back (see the top illustration on page 25.) To begin construction, start by cutting the pieces to length and width according to the materials list. Then, make full-sized patterns for the rear leg and seat support from the scale drawings on page 25.

1 Transfer the rear leg pattern onto the wood and cut the rear legs (A) to shape on the band saw. Instead of sanding the edges smooth, you'll end up with a flatter surface if you plane them. Clamp the leg in a vise and use a jack plane to smooth the edges, taking care to plane with the grain. When the rear legs are done, cut the front legs (B) to size.

2 The next step is to lay out matching mortises on the front and rear legs for the arms, seat supports and bottom rails. Also lay out matching mortises on the front legs for the front stretcher, and on the rear legs for the bottom stretcher and the back top and bottom. Remember: You're making a book-matched set here since there is a right and a left side. When the mortises are laid out, use the mortising jig (shown on page 122) to rout ³⁄₄-inch-wide, 2-inch-deep mortises. Note that the mortises for the front and back stretchers and back top and bottom are ¹⁄₂ inch wide and 1¹⁄₈ inches deep. Cut tenons on the seat supports (D) and bottom rails (E) to fit the mortises. You'll also need to cut a ³⁄₄-inch-wide, 1-inch-long tenon on the top of each front leg for the arms (you'll cut these mortises later).

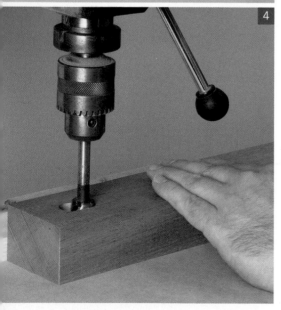

3 After the tenons are cut and the joints are fitted, use the seat support pattern to lay out the curve on the seat supports. Then cut the seat supports to shape and sand the curves smooth with a drum sander.

4 Cut the arms (C) to size and lay out mortises on the bottom of each arm. The simplest way to cut these is to drill out the waste with a Forstner bit in a drill press and then square up the mortise with a chisel.

5 Each 2¹⁄₂-inch-wide arm tapers towards the rear, where it's joined to a rear leg. To make this taper, make a mark ³⁄₈ inch in from the edge at the rear of the arm and draw a line from the front corner to the mark on each side. Cut the taper on the band saw and smooth the edges with a jack plane. Then cut an angled tenon on the back of the arm to fit into the mortise in the rear leg. Use a hand saw and then trim it to fit with a chisel. Go slowly, paring away a little at a time. Next, lay out, cut, and sand a 1³⁄₄-inch-radius curve on the front end of each arm.

6 Dry-assemble each side one more time, and if everything fits well, rout a ⅛-inch chamfer on all edges. Then apply glue and clamp up each side.

7 After the glue dries, drill ¼-inch *stopped* holes for pegs to lock each mortise-and-tenon joint together. Drill on the *inside* faces centered on each tenon. Then drizzle some glue in the hole and drive a peg in place. When the glue dries, pare away any protruding peg with a sharp chisel.

8 To make the seat, first cut tenons on the ends of the front and back stretchers (G) to fit their respective mortises. Then lay out matching mortises on the inside faces of the stretchers for the middle seat support (F). Drill out the mortise waste on the drill press with a ¾-inch Forstner bit, and clean up the sides with a chisel. Next, lay out, cut, and sand the curve on the support and then cut tenons on the ends of the middle seat support to fit the mortises.

9 All that's left is to rout a ⅛-inch chamfer on the top edges of each slat, and lay out and drill countersunk pilot holes for screws at the ends and middle of each slat.

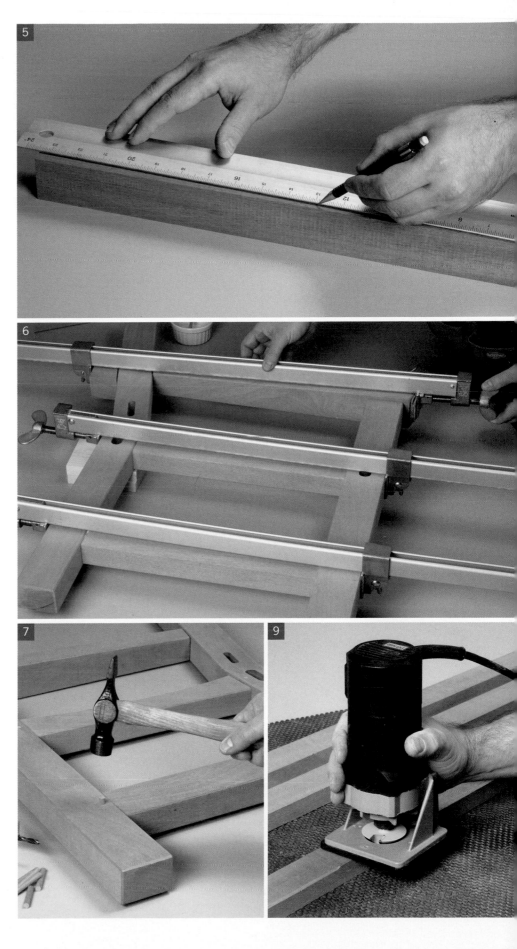

10 The arched back is the real challenge to this project: Curves just complicate things, especially when you need to cut a lot of mortises for slats. But we've made it easier to build by using faux mortises in the bottom stretcher and a simple slot in the top. The first step is to cut 1⅛-inch-long tenons on the ends of the back top and bottom (I, J) to fit mortises in the rear legs. Although this may seem out of sequence, it's much easier cutting tenons on the ends of square versus curved parts.

11 Although you could create the curve for the back with a bent stick, you can also let Mother Nature provide the curve via gravity. To make a gravity curve, drape a chain or string from one end of a scrap of plywood or hardboard that measures 57¾ inches long and 7 inches wide. Drape the chain or string so that the bottom of the arch hits the center of the board; then carefully trace around the string/chain. Then cut out the template curve and transfer this to the back top (I). Cut the curve on the back top to shape; then sand or plane it smooth.

12 To define the bottom edge of the arch, set a divider to 3 inches and use it to trace a curve parallel to the first curve. Run the point of the divider along the side of the curve and the pencil will draw a perfectly parallel curved line. Cut the bottom of the arch and sand the curve smooth.

13 Once the arch is cut, rout a ⅜-inch-wide groove centered in the bottom edge of the back top with a slot cutter. This slot will house the tops of the slats. Next, on the table saw, cut a ⅜-inch-wide groove centered in the top edge of the back bottom with a dado blade. This slot accepts the slat bottoms and plugs. To complete the back top and bottom, trim the tenons to fit the mortises in the back legs.

14 Cut the back slats to rough length, as shown in the illustration at right. Insert the slats in the back bottom beginning with the center slat and then space them 1⅝ inches apart. Next, to mark the slats to match the arch, lay the back top on the slats. To ensure that the slats will be the correct length, position the top so the tenons on the ends of the back top and bottom are the correct distance from each other plus ½ inch to allow for the slot in the top. Then mark the curve on the slats.

SLAT LENGTH

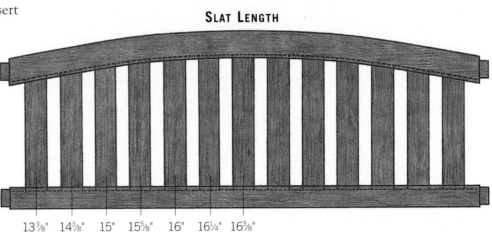

13⅜" 14⅜" 15" 15⅝" 16" 16¼" 16⅜"

15 Now cut the curves on the slat tops and dry-assemble the back and the sides with the slats in place. Cut ⅜-inch-wide, ½-inch-deep plugs to a length of 1⅝ inches to fit into the back bottom, and set them aside. To assemble the bench, glue the slats into the back top and bottom using the plugs to space them correctly. Center the center slat and work out toward the ends.

Apply glue to the tenons of the back/front stretchers, and the back top and bottom, and assemble with clamps. (Note: You'll need clamps at least 6 feet long here.) Finally, attach the seat slats (H) to the seat supports with #8 × 1½-inch screws. Because of the arms, you'll need to drive in the end screws with a "stubby" screwdriver or use a right-angle driver/drill. Sand the entire project with 150-grit sandpaper and apply the finish of your choice.

curved-back bench

If just looking at an airline seat gives you a backache, you'll appreciate the lumbar support of this deceptively simple-looking beauty. Once you've built it, you can really relax in this one.

- **Material: Teak**
- **Adhesive: Epoxy**
- **Finish: Teak oil**
- **Level: Challenging**

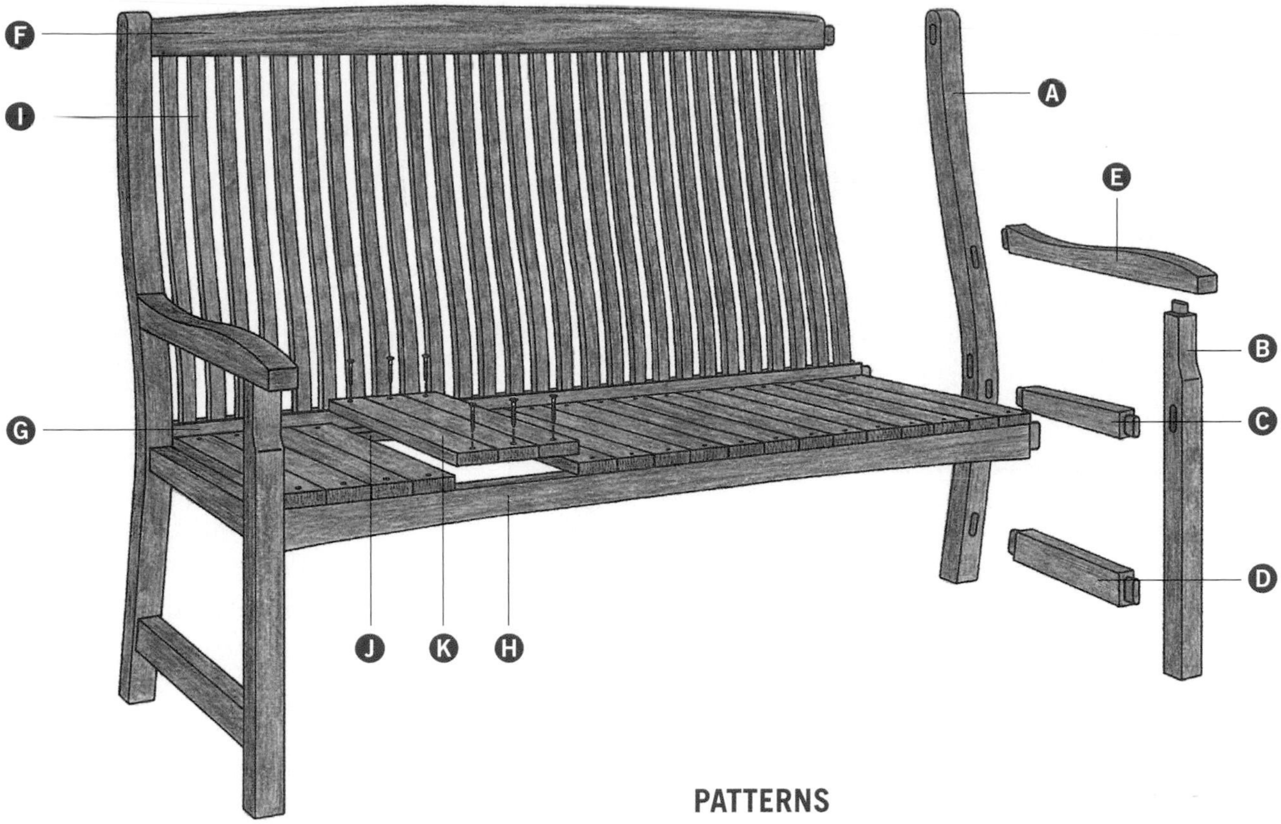

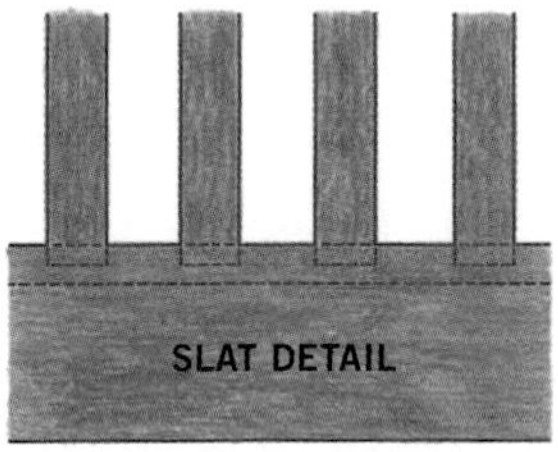

PATTERNS

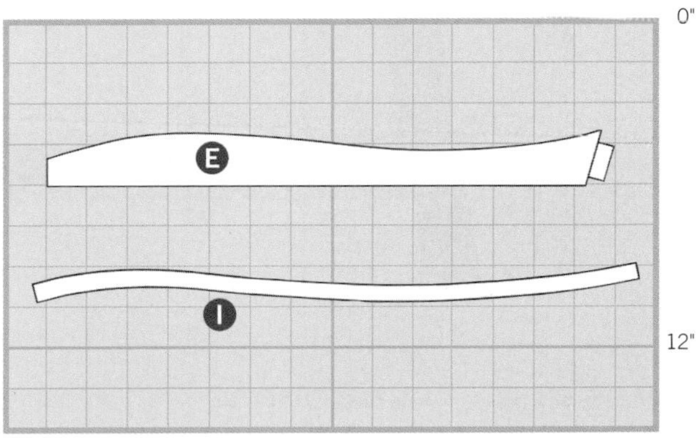

One square = 1½"

Here's one to exercise your skills: This seemingly simple bench is the most challenging project in this book. Although the joinery is straightforward mortise-and-tenon, the tough part is making a series of perfectly matching curved pieces for the back slats. But with a production technique called pattern routing, you can duplicate these curved parts with ease. (For more on this, see the routing jig on page 36.)

MATERIALS LIST

PART	NAME	QUANTITY	DIMENSIONS
A	Rear legs	2	1¾" × 40" – 8/4 stock
B	Front legs	2	1¾" × 23" – 8/4 stock
C	Seat stretchers	2	1¾" × 16⅝" – 8/4 stock
D	Bottom stretchers	2	2" × 18⅝" – 8/4 stock
E	Arms	2	1¾" × 21" – 8/4 stock
F	Top rail	1	3" × 48" – 5/4 stock
G	Bottom rail	1	2½" × 48" – 5/4 stock
H	Front rail	1	2½" × 48" – 5/4 stock
I	Back slats	26	¾" × 22½" – ¾" stock
J	Seat support	1	1⅛" × 46" – 5/4 stock
K	Seat slats	20	2⅛" × 17" – ¾" stock

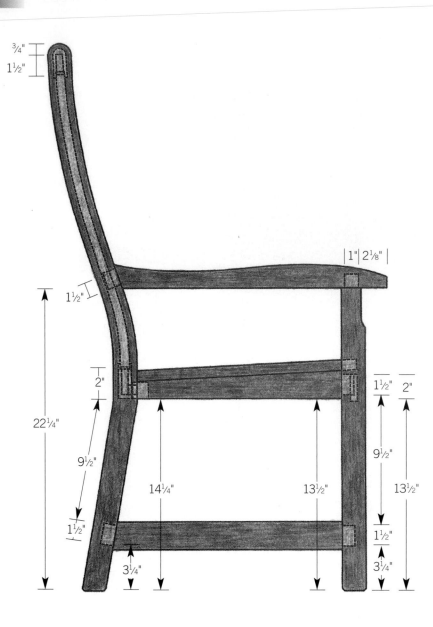

¾"
1½"

1" 2⅛"

1½"

2"

22¼"

9½"

1½"

14¼"

13½"

1½" 2"

9½"

13½"

1½"

3¼"

3¼"

Assembly Instructions

The curved-back bench consists of two side assemblies connected with three rails. A set of curved slats make up the back and fit into faux mortises. The seat also is made up of slats that are screwed in place (see the top illustration on page 31). To start, cut the parts to width and length according to the materials list. Then make full-sized patterns for the arms, front and rear legs, plus the back slats, from the scale drawings on page 31 and above).

1 Each side assembly consists of a rear and front leg, arm, and seat and bottom stretcher. All of the pieces are joined together with mortise-and-tenon joints. Transfer the rear leg pattern onto the wood by tracing around it; if

you nestle two together, you can get them both out of a single blank that's 7⅞ inches wide. Note: For darker woods like teak, it's often easier to see your layout lines if you use a white pencil as shown.

2 Then cut the rear legs (A) to rough shape on the band saw or with a saber saw, and sand the edges smooth with a drum sander mounted in a drill press or in a portable drill. Next, cut the front legs (B) to size, and lay out the slight indent on the top of each piece. Cut the shape and sand it smooth.

3 Once the front and rear legs are shaped, lay out matching mortises on the *inside* faces of each rear leg for the top and bottom rails (see the illustration at left). Also, lay out matching mortises on the front edges of the rear legs and the back edges of the front legs for the arm, seat stretcher, and bottom stretcher. Finally, lay out matching mortises on the *inside* faces of the front legs for the front rail and the rear legs for the top and bottom rail.

4 Use the self-centering mortising jig shown on page 122 to rout all mortises. Clamp the workpiece firmly to your bench, and cut each mortise by taking a series of light cuts. Note: All leg mortises are ¾ inch wide and 1 inch deep. The top, bottom, and front rail mortises are ½ inch wide and 1 inch deep. Since the top rail mortise is so close to the end of the rear leg, you can't use the mortising jig here because the guide pins will slip off the end before completing the cut. Instead, you'll need to drill out the waste with a Forstner bit and clean up the sides with a sharp chisel.

6 All that's left to complete the side assemblies is to add the arms (E). Begin by transferring the arm pattern to the arm blanks; cut them to shape and sand them smooth. Cut the angled tenon (about 14 degrees) on the back end of the arm to fit the mortise in the rear leg. Then lay out and cut the mortises in the underside of the arms to accept the tenons on the ends of the front legs. Next, cut the tenons on the top ends of the front legs to fit the mortises in the arms. Check the fit.

5 With the legs complete, the next step is to connect them with the stretchers and the arms. Cut the seat stretcher (C) and bottom stretcher (D) to rough size, and then angle the back end of the bottom stretcher to match the angle of the rear leg (about 7½ degrees). Cut tenons on the ends of all four stretchers to fit their respective mortises. The quickest way to cut these is with a dado blade in the table saw. Use the miter gauge to guide the cut, and set the rip fence as a stop to define the shoulders of the tenon. You will have to either round over the tenons or square up the mortises for the parts to fit. Next, lay out and cut a taper on the seat stretcher (1¾ inches on one end, tapering to 1¼ inches on the opposite end). Dry-assemble the legs and stretchers to check the fit, and then fine-tune any joints as necessary.

7 Dry-assemble each side one more time. If everything fits well, apply glue, and clamp up each side assembly. Note: If you're using epoxy, make sure to use the slower-setting type; 5-minute epoxy doesn't provide enough time to apply glue and assemble everything before it sets up.

8 The side assemblies are connected with three rails: a top (F) and bottom (G) rail for the back, and one in front (H). Cut tenons on the ends of each rail to fit their respective mortises. Then to accept the "mortise" strip for the back slats, cut a ⅝-inch-wide, ½-inch-deep groove along the *inside* edges of the top and bottom rail. Use a straight bit in a router table or a dado blade in the table saw, as shown here. Adjust the rip fence for a centered cut, and use a featherboard to press the rail firmly against the rip fence.

9 Next, lay out a gradual curve on the top of the top rail and the bottom of the front rail. Clamp a thin strip of wood in place and trace along the strip with a pencil. The curve on the top rail begins 1 inch down from each end; the height of the curve on the front rail is centered ¾ inch up from the bottom of the rail. Once you've laid out the curves, cut them to shape and sand them smooth. Then rout a ½-inch round-over on the top edges of the top rail.

10 To create mortises for the back slats, cut a "no-mortise" strip to fit in the grooves in the top and bottom rails as described on page 123. The notches for the mortises are ¾ inch wide and spaced 1 inch apart. Trim the strips to fit the grooves, and glue and clamp them in place. When the epoxy has set, dry-assemble the bench and check to make sure the pattern you made for the back slats fits perfectly between the rails; adjust as necessary.

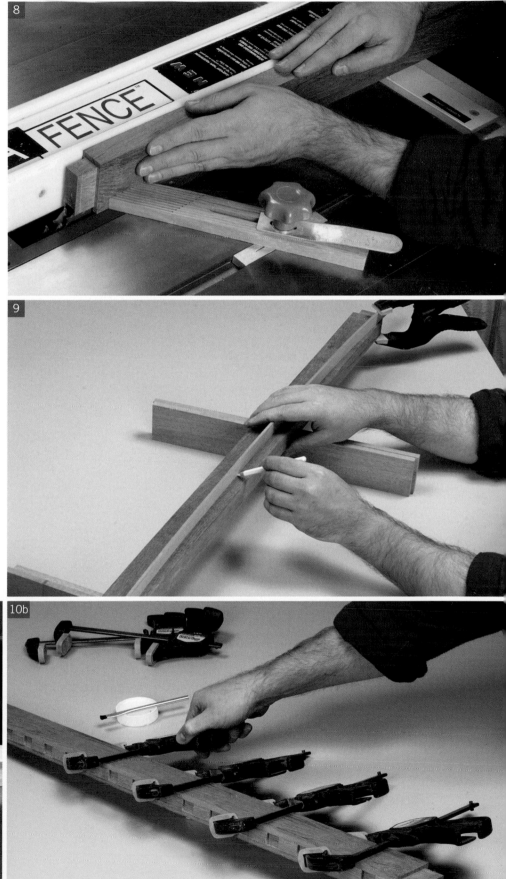

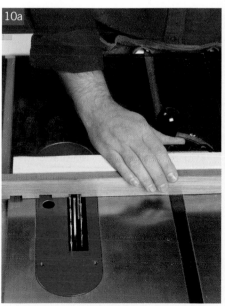

11 And now for the fun part: making a set of perfectly matched, curved back slats. Transfer the slat pattern to the wood—you can get five slats out of a 5½-inch-wide board if you nestle them together. It's a good idea to cut a few extra in case of chip-out when routing, or to better match grain patterns. Rough-cut the slats (I) to size, leaving about 1/16 to 1/8 inch waste. It's not critical to hit exactly 1/16 inch; what is important is that the waste be fairly consistent in width so the blank can be positioned properly on the routing jig.

12 Build the routing jig as described below. Insert a rough blank in the jig and rout it to shape, using a patternmaker's bit mounted in a router table. Then move the routed piece to the front of the jig, insert a new blank, and rout both pieces. Continue this way until all slats are routed. Soften the edges of the slats with sandpaper and check the fit in the mortises. Alternatively, you can sand the curved slats to final shape.

13 Dry-assemble the bench one more time. If everything fits, start by applying glue to the mortises for the slats. Assemble the top and bottom rails with slats and hold them together with clamps or twine. Apply glue to the tenons on one end on the assembled back, and fit them into the appropriate side assembly. Apply glue and insert the front rail. Then spread glue on the remaining tenons and clamp the opposite side assembly in place.

14 When the glue has set, remove the clamps. Attach the seat support (J) flush to the bottom inside edge of the bottom rail with glue and screws.

15 To complete the bench, rout a 1/8-inch chamfer on all top edges of the seat slats (K) and drill countersunk pilot holes 5/8 inch in from both ends and centered on each slat. Position the slats for even gaps, and screw them to the seat support and front rail with #8 × 1¼-inch screws. Sand the entire project with 150-grit sandpaper, and apply the finish of your choice.

Production Routing Jig

This routing jig lets you make perfectly identical curved slats. The front and back edges of the base of the jig are shaped to match the front and back curves of the slats (one curve on each side). A patternmaker's bit follows these curves and routs the blanks clamped in place on the jig. Clamping pressure is supplied by two sets of specialty clamps called "toggle" clamps, available from most woodworking mail-order companies. These are used in industry for repetitive work, as they allow for quick clamping and unclamping.

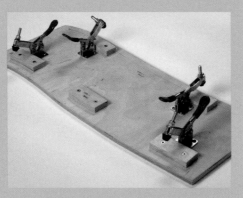

Use the vertical slat pattern to transfer the curves to the front and back edges of a 10-inch-wide, 24-inch-long piece of ½-inch-thick Baltic Birch (or other high-grade plywood). Take care to sand these curves smooth, as this will be the final shape of your slats. Position a rough blank over the back curve edge; then glue and screw a pair of support blocks to the jig. Next, screw the toggle clamps directly behind the support blocks and test the clamp. The rubber end of the clamp should compress to solidly

grip the blank. Rout the curve and then move this to the front curve and repeat the support block/clamp procedure to position the blank. Once set up, you can rout two slats at a time.

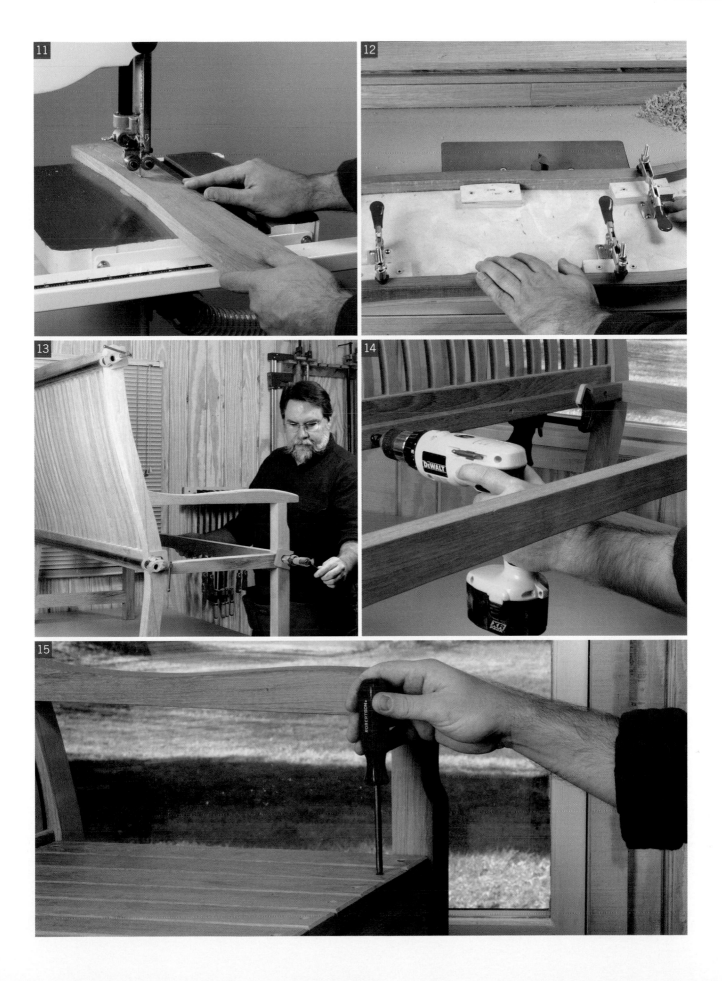

rocking bench

Come and rock awhile. The invitation is irresistible when this project graces your garden or patio. Good lumbar support for the body; clean, flowing lines for the eye; and the relaxing rhythm of rocking on a summer night for the spirit.

- **Material:** Teak
- **Adhesive:** Epoxy
- **Finish:** Teak oil
- **Level:** Moderate

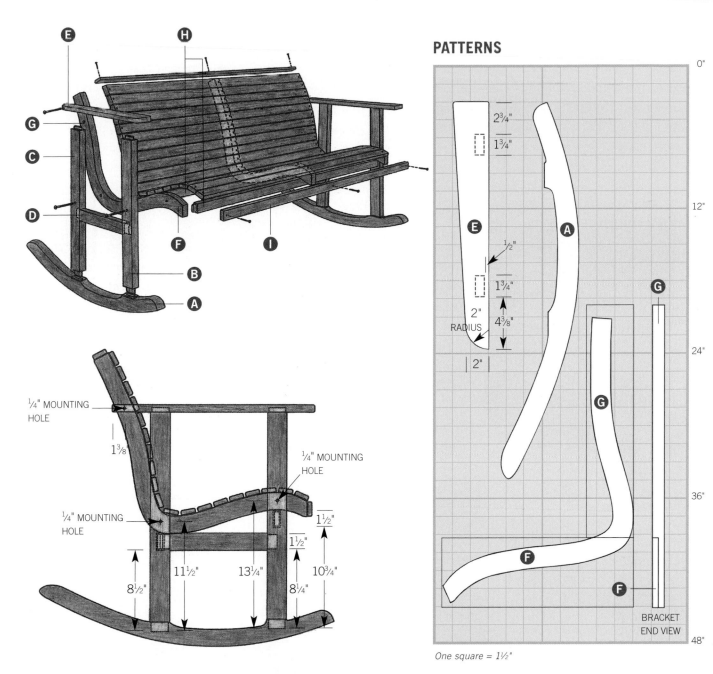

PATTERNS

One square = 1½"

With its multiple curves and multiple slats, this one may look more difficult than it is. Actually, a moderate skill level will move you readily through the process: A straightforward and sturdy base supports three curved seat brackets. After the frame is complete, you just screw on the slats to create a surprisingly comfortable rocking bench. Invest a few afternoons in outdoor ease that can last for decades.

MATERIALS LIST

PART	NAME	QUANTITY	DIMENSIONS
A	Rockers	2	2" × 32" – ⁸⁄₄ stock
B	Front legs	2	2" × 22³⁄₄" – 1½" stock
C	Back legs	2	2" × 23" – 1½" stock
D	Side rails	2	2" × 12" – ³⁄₄" stock
E	Arms	2	3" × 20³⁄₄" – ³⁄₄" stock
F	Short brackets	3	5³⁄₄" × 16" – ⁵⁄₄ stock
G	Long brackets	3	4" × 25" – ⁵⁄₄ stock
H	Stretchers	2	1³⁄₄" × 50" – ⁵⁄₄ stock
I	Slats	21	1½" × 48" – ½" stock

Assembly Instructions

The rocking bench features a pair of side assemblies with rockers connected by two stretchers (see the top illustration on page 39). Curved seat brackets attach to the sides and hold slats that form the seat and back. Each side is made up of a front and rear leg, a rocker, a side rail, and an arm. To begin, cut the parts to width and length according to the materials list. Then create full-sized patterns for the rocker, arm, and seat brackets from the scale drawing on page 39.

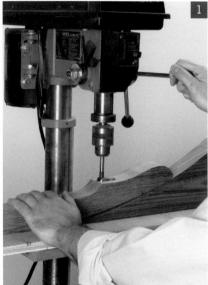

1 Start work on the sides by making the rockers (A). Transfer the rocker template to a rough blank; you can get two rockers from a blank that's 7 inches × 41 inches. Then cut the rockers to shape on the band saw. Make sure to save the scraps—you'll need them to drill the mortises. Sand the rockers smooth and then lay out the mortise locations. Drill 1-inch-deep mortises using a ¾-inch Forstner bit to make a series of overlapping holes. Use the scraps you saved to level the rocker for drilling. Adjust the scraps so the drill bit is perpendicular to the flat portions of the rocker where the legs attach. When done, clean up the sides of the mortises with a chisel.

2 The next step is to make the front and back legs (B, C). Cut tenons on the bottom end of each part to fit the mortises in the rockers. Then cut ¾-inch-wide, ½-inch-long tenons on top of each piece for the mortises that will be cut in the arms. Next, lay out mortises for the side rails (D) and stretchers (H), making sure to create bookmatched pairs.

3 Now rout mortises in both pairs of front and back legs with the mortising jig shown on page 122. Then lay out and drill ¼-inch-diameter mounting holes in the legs that you'll use later to attach the seat bracket. (See the detail drawing on page 39 for hole locations.)

4 The tops of the legs are connected with side rails (D) at about their midpoint and with arms (E) on top. Cut 1-inch-long, ½-inch-wide tenons on the ends of the side rails to fit the mortises in the legs; round over the tenons, or square up the mortises. Then use the arm template to transfer the shape to the arm blanks. Cut them out on the band saw and sand the edges smooth.

5 Next, lay out the mortises in the underside of each arm— again, you're making a matched pair here. The most accurate way to do this is to dry-assemble each side and then butt the arm up against the tenons on the front and rear legs and mark their locations directly on the bottom of the arm. Then drill ½-inch-deep mortises at the drill press and clean up the sides with a chisel. Finally, rout a ⅛-inch round-over on all parts of the side assembly.

6 To assemble the sides, first dry-fit the parts with clamps to check the fit, and adjust as necessary. When everything goes together well, apply glue to the ends of the tenons, connect the parts, and apply clamps.

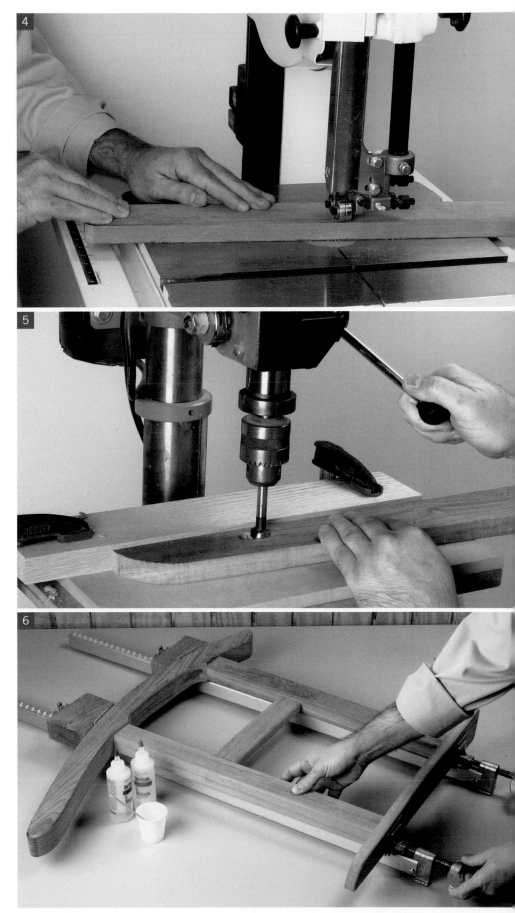

7 With the side assemblies complete, the next step is to make the curved seat brackets. Each bracket starts out as a short and long bracket (F, G), glued up to form an "L". The ends of the brackets are rabbeted to form a half-lap joint. When glued together this creates an overlapping grain pattern that yields a strong bracket. Cut the rabbets using a dado set on the table saw. Use the miter gauge to guide the workpiece, and set the rip fence to define the shoulder of the rabbet.

8 Glue pairs of brackets together to create the "L" shape. It's a good idea to protect your work surface with a drop cloth and to use a scrap block under the clamp heads to help evenly distribute pressure.

9 When the glue is dry on all three brackets, use the seat bracket template to transfer the shape onto the L-brackets. Then cut the brackets to shape on the band saw or with a saber saw, and sand the edges smooth.

10 To assemble the rocking bench, start by cutting ½-inch-wide, 1-inch-long tenons on the ends of the stretchers (H) to fit the mortises in the legs; round over the tenons or square up the mortises. Then apply glue to the tenons and clamp the stretchers between the sides.

11 Next, position the end seat brackets on the stretchers and temporarily clamp them in place so the front end of each bracket extends 1¾ inches past the front stretcher. Then drill through the holes you previously drilled in the legs and into and through the seat brackets. You'll also need to drill through the back ends of the arms and into and through the seat brackets. Secure the brackets with ¼-inch × 3-inch bolts, nuts, and washers.

12 All that's left is to add the center bracket and the slats. Start by attaching two slats (I) to the top and front of the end seat brackets with #8 × 1½-inch screws. Then center the remaining seat bracket on the stretchers, and attach it to the two slats you just installed. Finally, position the remaining slats with even gaps and secure them with #8 × 1½-inch screws. Sand the entire project with 150-grit sandpaper, and apply the finish of your choice.

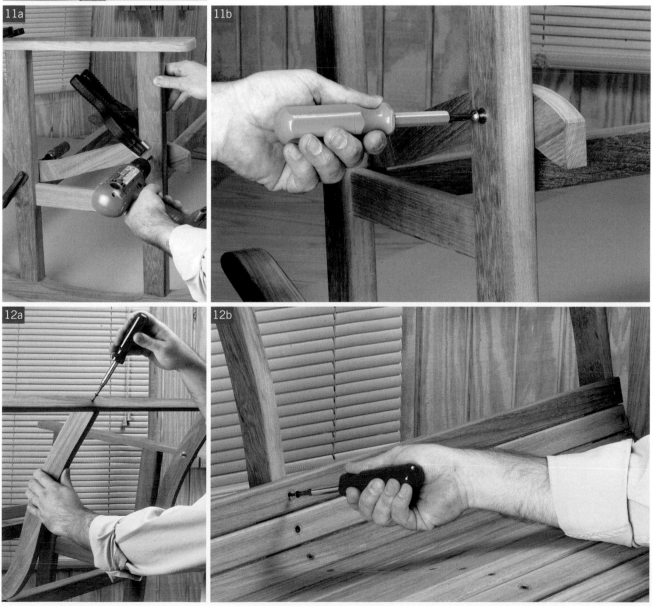

planter bench

Plant yourself—and some colorful potted plants—here, in a versatile planter/bench. It's perfect for patios or anywhere you need extra seating. Built-in planters provide plenty of room for arranging your favorite plants.

- **Material:** Redwood
- **Adhesive:** Resorcinol
- **Finish:** 2 coats of satin spar varnish
- **Level:** Moderate

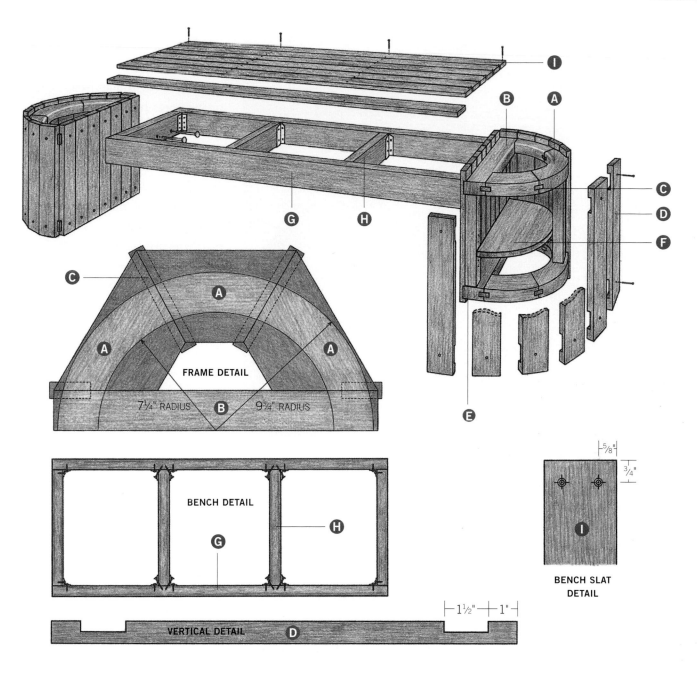

FRAME DETAIL

7¼" RADIUS   9¾" RADIUS

BENCH DETAIL

BENCH SLAT
DETAIL

VERTICAL DETAIL

At first, this distinctive piece may look intimidating, but it's easier to make than you might think. Constructing the half-round planters that "bookend" the bench is actually simple—kind of like building with Lincoln Logs. And it has a special feature that lets you show off plants to their best advantage: Inside each planter is a shelf that adjusts up and down, so you can display almost any potted plant at the perfect height.

MATERIALS LIST

PART	NAME	QUANTITY	DIMENSIONS
A	Frame sides	12	5½" × 10" – 1½" stock
B	Frame backs	4	2½" × 20" – 1½" stock
C	Splines	16	1" × 7" – ½" stock
D	Vertical slats	38	2⁷⁄₁₆" × 16" – ¾" stock
E	Shelf supports	6	1½" × 11³⁄₈" – 1½" stock
F	Adjustable shelves	2	8" × 16" – ¾" stock
G	Bench front/back	2	3½" × 46" – 1½" stock
H	Bench rails	4	3½" × 16" – 1½" stock
I	Bench slats	7	2½" × 45¾" – ¾" stock

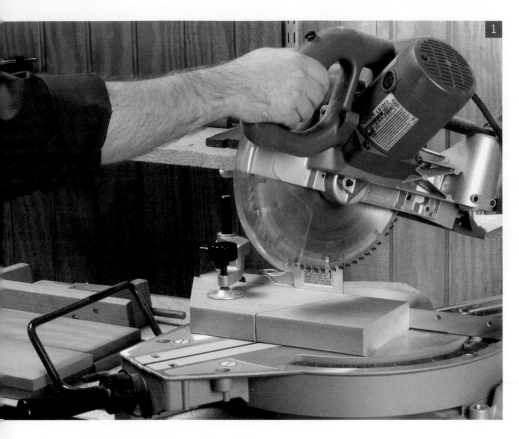

Assembly Instructions

The planter stand consists of three assemblies: one bench supported by two matching curved planters (see the top illustration on page 45). Each planter consists of a pair of curved frames that accept a set of vertical slats. The bench is 2 × material held together with joist hangers and brackets, and topped with slats. The units are then bolted together to create a sturdy bench. To start construction, begin by cutting the parts to width and length according to the materials list.

1 To make the planters, start by making the frames: Each consists of three mitered sides (A) and a rectangular back (B). The ends of the pieces are grooved and joined together with splines. Miter the ends of the frame sides (A) to 30 degrees.

2 The splines fit in grooves that are routed in both ends of the sides and in the ends of each back. Although you can cut these grooves on the table saw, it's easier to rout them using a slot cutter in a table-mounted router. Rout a ½-inch-wide slot in the ends of each frame side, centered on the thickness of the side.

3 The grooves on the backs are *stopped* grooves; that is, they don't run the full width of the back, but instead stop a set distance in from the end. Temporarily clamp a scrap to the router fence to create a 2¼-inch-long groove, ½ inch wide and centered on the thickness of the back.

4 The next step is to make the splines (C) that fit in the grooves in the frame pieces. Cut or thickness-plane 5½-inch-wide stock to ½-inch thickness. It's important to note the orientation of the grain as you do this. What you want is the grain to run across the *width* of the spline and not the length. This creates a spline that will not split or crack if stressed. If you were to orient the grain in the opposite direction, the spline would be extremely weak. Cut the splines to a width of 1 inch on the table saw.

5 Now you can assemble each of the four frames with glue and splines. The best way to hold the frame parts together as the glue dries is to use a band clamp, as shown.

6 When all the frames are dry, lay out a 9¾-inch radius to create the arch. You can use a trammel point as shown; or simply drill a pair of holes 9¾ inches apart in a thin strip of wood and then drive a nail in the center-point of the back frame and insert a pencil in the opposite hole to scribe the arc. Next, lay out the inside curve 2½ inches in from the outer curve. Now cut the outside curve on the band saw or with a saber saw, and then cut the inside curve with a saber saw. Sand the inside and outside curves smooth. Finally, rout a ⅜-inch round-over on the *inside* top edges of two of the frames.

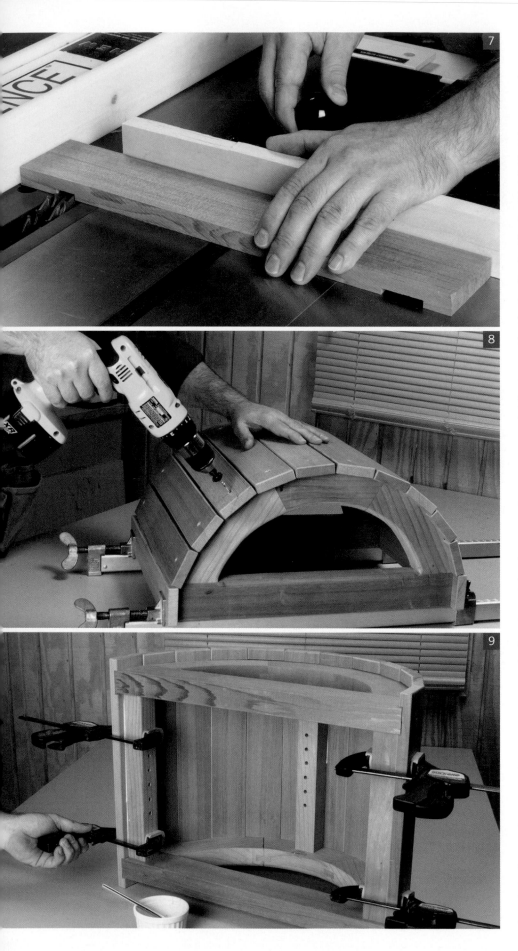

7 With the frames complete, work can begin on the vertical slats (D). First, cut a 1½-inch-wide, ⅜-inch-deep dado 1 inch down from the top and bottom edge of each slat. These notches slip over the frames to lock the slats in place. A dado blade fitted in a table saw is the quickest way to do this. Use the miter gauge to guide the slat and set the rip fence to define the shoulders of the dadoes. Then drill centered, countersunk pilot holes in the top and bottom of each slat for the screws that you'll use to affix the slats to the frames. To soften the edges of the slats and help prevent splintering, rout a ⅛-inch round-over on all front edges.

8 Each planter section is assembled by first attaching slats to the curved portions of the frames. Take care to position a frame with the rounded-over inside edges as the top for each planter. Use a pair of bar clamps to temporarily hold the end slats in place, drill pilot holes, and secure the vertical slats to the frames with #8 × 1¾-inch screws.

9 Before you attach slats to the back of the planter, there's one more thing to do: Make and install the supports that fit inside the planter to hold the shelves. Drill a series of ¼-inch centered holes for shelf pins in the shelf supports (E), starting 3 inches up from the bottom and every 1 inch, for a total of six holes. Then glue these inside the planter—two supports ½ inch in from the ends, and one centered on the curve. Now attach slats to enclose the back. If necessary, spread these slats apart to create even gaps.

10 The adjustable shelves (F) sit on metal shelf pins fitted into the holes in the supports. To make the shelves, glue up sufficient stock to create two 8-inch × 16-inch blanks. Then lay out an 18-inch radius, cut the shelves to size, and sand the edges smooth.

11 The planters are spanned by a bench made up of 2 × 4 pieces: a front and back (G) and four rails (H). The end rails are joined to the front and back with L-brackets and screws; the center rails attach via joist hangers.

12 To attach the bench to the planters, first clamp the bench in place so the top edge of the bench frame is 2 inches down from the top of the planters. Then drill $^5\!/_{16}$-inch holes for carriage bolts through the bench frame and into the planter backs. Bolt the assemblies together with $^5\!/_{16}$-inch × 3-inch galvanized carriage bolts, washers, and nuts.

13 Now add the bench slats (I). Start by routing or sanding a $^1\!/_8$-inch round-over on the top edges of each of the slats. Then drill countersunk pilot holes $^3\!/_4$ inch in from the ends and centered on the rails (H). Secure the slats to the bench with #8 × $1^3\!/_4$-inch screws. Sand with 150-grit sandpaper, and apply a finish.

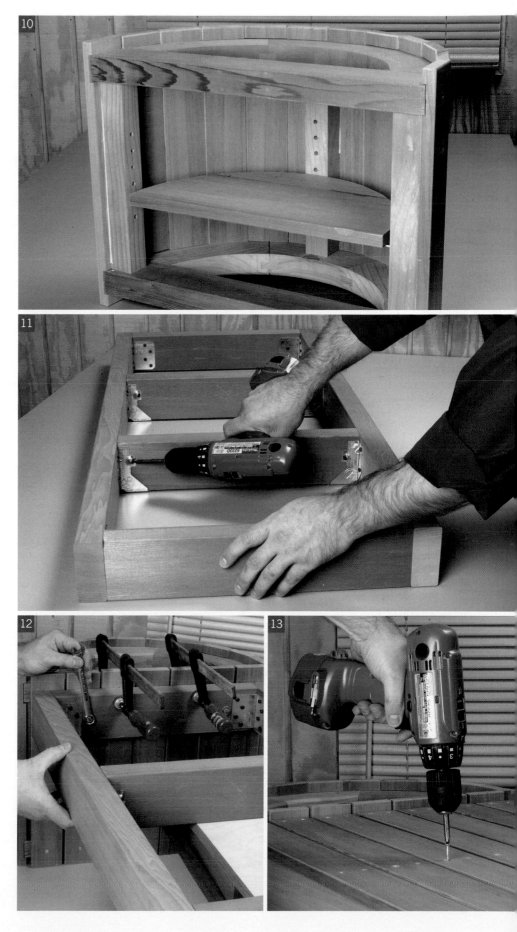

sunburst arbor bench

Want to curl up with a good book under the shade of vining plants? This pergola-and-bench combo supports both you and a canopy of greenery. Or, skip the plants and leave the sunburst design uncovered.

- **Material:** Redwood and cedar
- **Adhesive:** Resorcinol or Titebond II
- **Finish:** Water sealant
- **Level:** Moderate

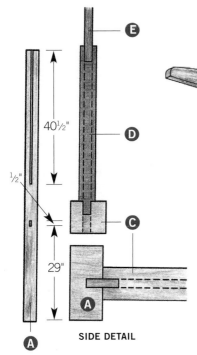

SIDE DETAIL

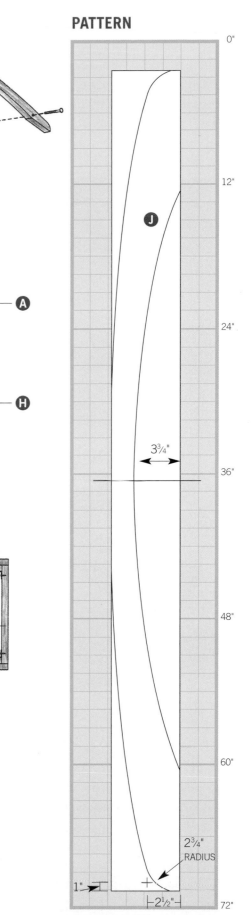

PATTERN

0"

12"

24"

3³⁄₄"

36"

48"

60"

2³⁄₄"
RADIUS

1"

2¹⁄₂"

72"

One square = 1¹⁄₂"

Tailor this striking arbor bench to your skills. The sunburst panel is the only real challenge here, and you can omit it if you like, for building ease. The main assemblies simply bolt together for sturdiness, while the wide seat allows you and a companion to enjoy some sheltered time. Achieve the two-tone effect with redwood and cedar, and leave unfinished, if you like, for a natural look.

BENCH DETAIL

MATERIALS LIST

PART	NAME	QUANTITY	DIMENSIONS
A	Posts	4	3¹⁄₂" ¥ 82" – 1¹⁄₂" stock
B	Side tops	2	3¹⁄₂" ¥ 27" – 1¹⁄₂" stock
C	Side rails	4	1¹⁄₂" ¥ 24" – 1¹⁄₂" stock
D	Sunburst centers	2	8" ¥ 14" – ³⁄₄" stock
E	Sunburst strips	46	³⁄₄" ¥ various lengths – ³⁄₈" stock
F	Bench front/back	2	5¹⁄₂" ¥ 48" – 1¹⁄₂" stock
G	Bench sides	2	5¹⁄₂" ¥ 24" – 1¹⁄₂" stock
H	Bench support	1	5¹⁄₂" ¥ 21" – 1¹⁄₂" stock
I	Bench slats	4	5¹⁄₂" ¥ 51" – ³⁄₄" stock
J	Arches	2	5¹⁄₂" ¥ 68" – 1¹⁄₂" stock
K	Top strips	11	³⁄₄" ¥ 30³⁄₄" – ³⁄₈" stock

Assembly Instructions

The sunburst arbor bench consists of two side assemblies with the sunburst design that are connected with a bench near the bottom and a pair of arches at the top. Strips are fastened to the arches to provide partial relief from the sun (and support for plants, if you choose). To start, cut the parts to width and length according to the materials list on page 51.

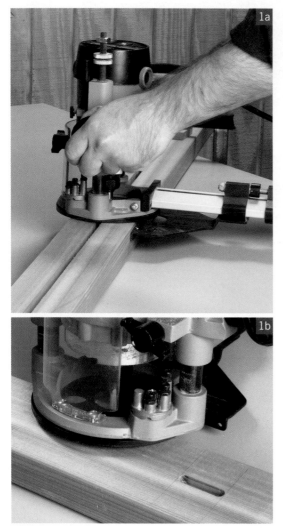

1 The first step in making the side assemblies is to rout ⅜-inch-wide, ¾-inch-deep grooves to house the sunburst center and the strips in the four posts (A). (See the left detail drawing on page 51.) The grooves are centered on the width of the stock and are 40½ inches long. The best way to rout these is to use an edge guide with the router fitted with a ⅜-inch straight bit. Next, lay out and rout mortises for the lower side rails; square up the corners of the mortises and the ends of the grooves with a sharp chisel.

2 You'll also need to rout centered grooves on the width of each side top (B). You can cut these with the portable router and edge guide, or cut them with a table-mounted router as shown here. Also, cut full-length grooves in two of the four side rails (C) to accept the sunburst centers. Like the grooves in the posts, these are ⅜ inch wide, ¾ inch deep, and centered on the thickness of the rails.

3 Instead of cutting tenons on the ends of the rails, it's easier to use the same router setup and rout a ⅜-inch-wide, ¾-inch-deep groove on the *ends* of all four rails. These then form open mortises to accept "loose" tenons. The loose tenons are just ⅜-inch-thick, 1½-inch-long pieces that are glued into the ends of the rails.

4 To assemble each side, first apply glue to the ends of the loose tenons on the side rail and insert these in the posts. The rail without the groove goes in the lower mortise. The grooved rail fits into the bottom of the long grooves in the posts, with the groove facing up. Apply clamps and measure diagonals to make sure the sides glue up square. Then drill countersunk pilot holes and screw the side tops to the ends of the posts with 3½-inch-long screws so the groove is facing in.

5 The next step is to make the sunburst centers (D). Start by gluing up stock to create 8-inch × 14-inch blanks. Then lay out a 7-inch-radius circle 1 inch up from the center of each blank. Cut these to shape and sand the edges smooth. One end of the sunburst strips fit in the grooves you cut in the top and posts; the other ends fit into a groove cut in the curved edge of the sunburst center. Rout a ⅜-inch-wide groove centered in the thickness of the stock with a slot cutter in a table-mounted router.

6 Create a ⅜-inch-wide, ¾-inch-long tongue along the bottom of each sunburst center to fit in the grooves in the side rails (do this on the table saw or router table). In either case, you'll need to clamp a piece of scrap wood to the rip fence to prevent the blade or bit from cutting into your fence.

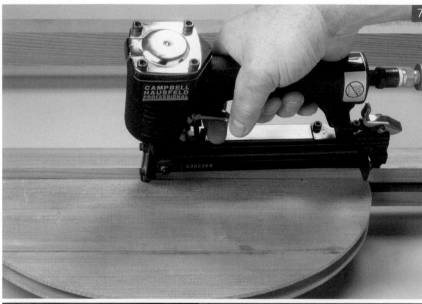

7 Now the sunburst center can be attached to the top side rail. Apply glue to the tongue and insert it centered in the side rail. Secure it with a couple of brads. Although we used a brad nailer, you can use a hammer and nails—just be sure the brads or nails are rated for outdoor use. Note: The advantage to an air nailer is it's extremely easy to nail at an angle. Just tilt the nailer and pull the trigger: It drives the brad in and sets it in the blink of an eye.

8 To complete the sides, add the strips (E). Cut ¾-inch stock to a width of ⅜ inch; 48-inch lengths work well. Start in the center and cut a strip to fit between the slot in the top and the sunburst center. Attach the strip at the top with a brad. Continue measuring and cutting strips to form the sunburst pattern. Typical spacing between strips is 1½ inches. When all strips are in place, drive a ½-inch brad through each slat where it fits into the sunburst center.

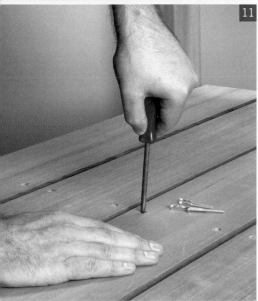

9 The bench is made up of a front and back (F), two sides (G), and a support (H). The parts are joined with L-brackets and joist hangers. Before you can install the L-brackets, you'll need to drill $7/16$-inch-diameter holes in them for the bolts that secure the side assemblies to the bench. Drill these holes $3/4$ inch in from the inside corner of each bracket and $7/8$ inch up from each end. Attach the bench sides to the fronts with the brackets you just drilled holes into; use #8 × $1\frac{1}{4}$-inch galvanized screws. Then add a joist hanger centered on the fronts, slip in the support (H), and secure it with the same screws.

10 To connect the side assemblies to the bench, temporarily clamp the bench between the sides and use a framing square to make sure the sides are perpendicular to the bench. Then drill $3/8$-inch holes through the holes you drilled in the brackets and into and through the posts. Next, add $3\frac{1}{2}$-inch-long carriage bolts with washers, and tighten the nuts.

11 With the sides attached, now you can add the bench slats (I). Lay out and drill countersunk pilot holes $3/4$ inch in from the corners of both ends and centered on the support (H). Secure the slats to the bench with #8 × $1\frac{1}{2}$-inch screws.

12 Use the pattern on page 51 to lay out the shape of the arches (J). Cut them to shape and sand the edges smooth. Clamp the arches to the tops of the sides so they protrude equally from each end and are flush with the tops of the sides. Then drill $3/8$-inch holes through the arches and through the sides. Bolt the parts together with $3\frac{1}{2}$-inch carriage bolts, nuts, and washers. Finally, attach the top strips (K) to the tops of the arches with brads so they're equally spaced and overhang the same distance.

potting stand

Form follows function here—with extras. Gardeners will appreciate the handy top shelf, with its pleasingly curved back edge, storage for pots and supplies, and the built-in soil-catcher. You will appreciate the ease of construction.

- **Material:** Cedar
- **Adhesive:** Titebond II
- **Finish:** 3 coats of satin spar varnish
- **Level:** Easy

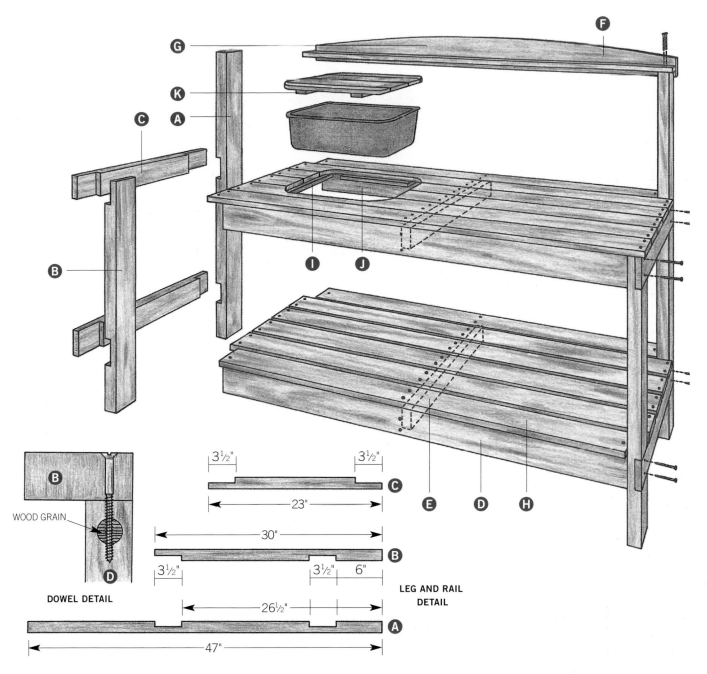

WOOD GRAIN

DOWEL DETAIL

3½"   3½"

23"

30"

3½"   3½"   6"

LEG AND RAIL
DETAIL

26½"

47"

Not a plant person yourself? If there's one in your life, she or he will love this project: Finally, it consolidates in one place all their plant pots, bags of soil, and accessories. This handy potting stand uses a nifty trick with hidden dowels that allows you to basically screw the project together. The remaining joinery is just as simple.

MATERIALS LIST

PART	NAME	QUANTITY	DIMENSIONS
A	Rear legs	2	3½" × 47" – 1½" stock
B	Front legs	2	3½" × 30" – 1½" stock
C	Rails	4	3½" × 23" – 1½" stock
D	Aprons	4	3½" × 46" – 1½" stock
E	Supports	2	3½" × 20" – 1½" stock
F	Top shelf	1	3½" × 50" – ¾" stock
G	Top	1	4½" × 50" – ¾" stock
H	Shelf slats	12	3½" × 49½" – ¾" stock
I	Side cleats	2	3½" × 21" – ¾" stock
J	Front/back cleats	2	3½" × 11½" – ¾" stock
K	Lid cleats	2	1½" × 12½" – ¾" stock

Assembly Instructions

The potting stand is made up of two side assemblies connected with a set of aprons beneath the top and bottom slats, and a narrow shelf and back on top (see the top illustration on page 57). A hole is cut in the top to accept a plastic dishpan; cleats under the top create a lip to support the container. The scraps left over from cutting the hole are used to create a lid. To begin construction, cut the parts to width and length according to the materials list.

1 Each side assembly consists of a front leg (A), a rear leg (B), and two rails (C). These parts are joined together with simple half-lap joints. Cut a ¾-inch-deep, 3½-inch-wide dado in the front and back legs for rails (see the detail drawing on page 57 for locations). Fit a dado blade in the table saw, use the miter gauge to guide the leg, and set the rip fence to define the shoulders of the dado.

2 Cut ¾-inch-deep, 3½-inch-wide rabbets on both ends of each rail to form the other half of the half-lap. Here again, use the miter gauge and rip fence.

3 Now test the fit of the half-laps. If everything goes together well, assemble the sides with glue and clamps. If you're using cedar (or another softwood), slip scraps of wood under the jaws of the clamps to keep the clamps from denting the wood as you apply pressure.

4 Although you could simply screw the side assemblies to the aprons (D), the screws won't have any holding power since they screw into end grain. Here's a nifty way to give the screws something to "bite" into and pull the parts securely together. Start by drilling centered, ¾-inch-diameter holes 1 inch in from the ends of the aprons on the *underside* of each

piece—3 inches deep. You can do this with a portable electric drill, but a drill press will drill a truly vertical hole. Then cut 3-inch lengths of ¾-inch dowel and glue them into the holes, taking care to orient the grain as shown in the detail drawing on page 57.

5 Once the glue has dried, temporarily clamp the aprons between the side assemblies and drill countersunk pilot holes for 3½-inch deck screws. Make sure the screws will penetrate into the center of the dowels in the aprons; then drive in the screws. Next, attach the supports (E) between pairs of aprons so they're centered from end to end. Here again, use the dowel trick from step 4 to give the screws more holding power.

6 Now you can add the parts that make up the top of the stand. Start by attaching the top shelf (F) to the tops of the rear legs with glue and screws, making sure to first drill countersunk pilot holes. Then lay out a gentle curve on the top (G), starting 2½ inches up from each end. Cut the curve to shape and sand the edges smooth. Next, temporarily clamp the top in place so it's centered on the top shelf, and secure it to the rear legs and to the top shelf with glue and screws.

7 With the stand beginning to take shape, the next step is to attach half of the shelf slats (H) to the lower apron and rails with screws. Before you do this, you'll need to trim the first and last slats to fit in between the sides. Then drill countersunk pilot holes ¾ inch in from the ends and centered on the support (E). Use ½-inch spacers between the slats to create even gaps, and secure the slats with #8 × 1½-inch screws.

8 If you don't want to add the soil container, attach the remaining slats to the top aprons and rails as you did with the bottom slats. To include the container, place the top slats on your work surface with the ends flush. Insert ½-inch spacers between the slats and temporarily clamp the top together. Position the container (we used a Rubbermaid dishpan) upside down on the top, and center from front to back about 6 inches in from the end. Scribe around the container with a pencil.

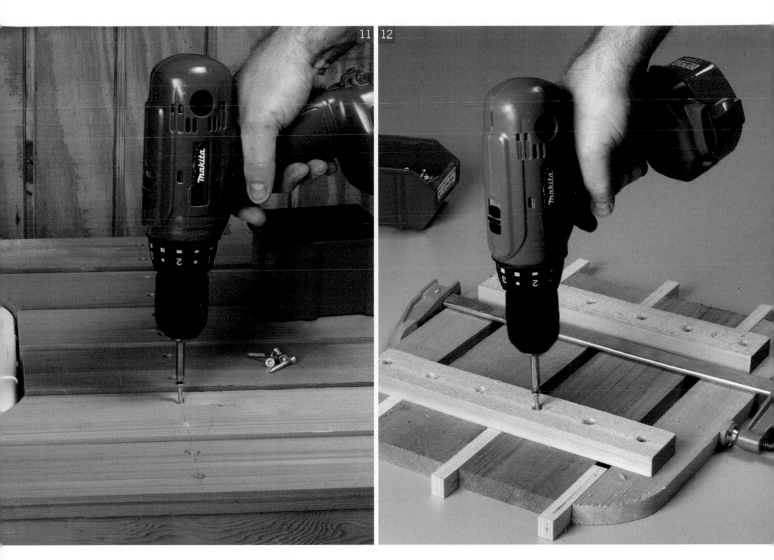

9 Before you cut the opening in the slats for the container, it's a good idea to number the slats so you can reassemble them in the proper order. Cut to the marked line with a band saw or saber saw, and sand the edges smooth. Make sure to save the pieces, as these will be used later to make the lid.

10 Reassemble the top slats upside down on your work surface with the spacers between the slats, and temporarily clamp the top together. Then attach the side, front, and back cleats (I, J) so they extend out into the opening and create a ½-inch-wide lip to catch the container. Drill countersunk pilot holes and attach the cleats with #8 × 1¼-inch screws.

11 Now you can flip the top unit over onto the stand and secure it with screws. Before you do this, you'll have to trim the last slat as you did for the bottom slats to fit between the sides. Make the overhang in the front and back equal, and then drill countersunk pilot holes. Secure the slats with #8 × 1½-inch screws.

12 All that's left is to make the lid to cover the container hole. Position the pieces you saved when cutting the opening in their correct order, and clamp ½-inch spacers between them. Then drill countersunk pilot holes in the lid cleats (K), and secure them to the slats with glue and #8 × 1¼-inch screws. Sand the project with 150-grit sandpaper, and apply the finish of your choice.

planter stands

Wood? No. Plastic? Not exactly. These durable planters are both handsome and hardy because they're made from plastic lumber. They'll be the finishing touch for porch, patio, or deck when you insert standard-sized container plants.

- **Material:** Plastic lumber
- **Adhesive:** Epoxy
- **Finish:** None required
- **Level:** Moderate

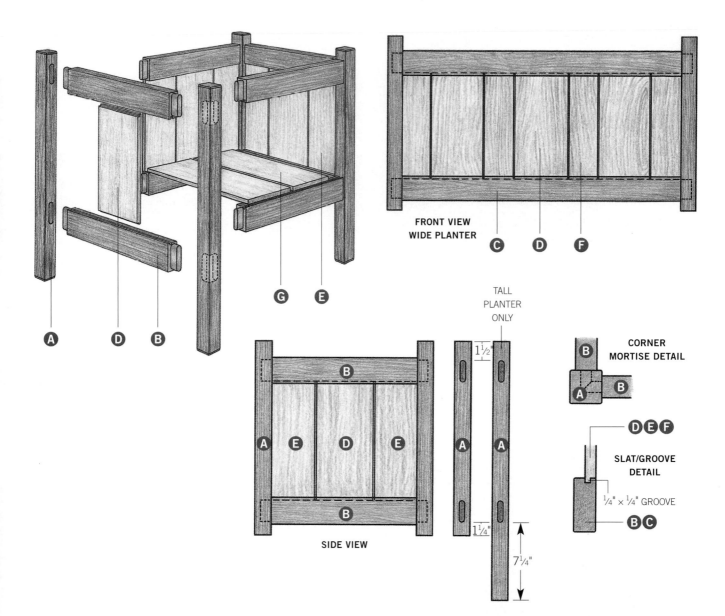

FRONT VIEW
WIDE PLANTER

Ⓒ Ⓓ Ⓕ

Ⓐ Ⓓ Ⓑ

Ⓖ Ⓔ

TALL
PLANTER
ONLY

1½"

1¼"

7¼"

Ⓑ
**CORNER
MORTISE DETAIL**
Ⓐ Ⓑ

Ⓑ
Ⓐ Ⓔ Ⓓ Ⓔ

ⒹⒺⒻ

**SLAT/GROOVE
DETAIL**

¼" × ¼" GROOVE

ⒷⒸ

Ⓑ

SIDE VIEW

Ⓐ Ⓐ

Here's where environmental concern meets appearance, courtesy of technology. Don't plunk plants on your patio in their original black plastic pots. Instead, place them in these attractive planters of plastic lumber, which is recycled plastic mixed with wood chips. This modern-day material is stable, is impervious to moisture, and won't fade or splinter. All three planters are based on the same design and all will hold a 13½-inch-diameter container.

MATERIALS LIST (for Tall, Short, and Wide Planters)

PART	NAME	QUANTITY	DIMENSIONS
A	Posts	4	1½" × 18" – 1½"-thick plastic lumber
			1½" × 24" – 1½"-thick plastic lumber
			(tall only)
B	Rails	8/4*	2½" × 15½" – 1"-thick plastic lumber
C	Long rails	4*	2½" × 30½" – 1"-thick plastic lumber
D	Wide slats	4/8*	5⅜" × 11" – ½" Timber Topper
E	Medium slats	8/4*	4" × 11" – ½" Timber Topper
F	Narrow slats	8*	3" × 11" – ½" Timber Topper
G	Bottom slats	2/4*	5½" × 14¾"† – 1"-thick plastic lumber

* wide planter
† rough dimension, cut to length
This materials list provides dimensions for all three planters. The tall and short planters differ only in the height of their posts.

Assembly Instructions

Each planter stand consists of four posts connected by eight rails. This "frame" is then filled with a combination of wide, medium, and narrow slats (see the top left illustration on page 63). The bottom is a series of slats that rests inside the frame. The instructions that follow are for the tall stand, but the procedure for the other stands is basically the same. Start by cutting the parts to width and length (with the exception of the slats), according to the materials list on page 63.

1 The posts (A) and rails (B) are joined with mortise-and-tenon joints. Begin by laying out centered, ½-inch-wide mortises on each post to create matching pairs (see the detail illustrations on page 63 for locations). A quick way to do this is to temporarily clamp the posts together and use a try square to mark them all at once.

2 Once the ends of the mortises are marked, clamp each post firmly to the workbench and use the mortising jig shown on page 122 to rout ½-inch-wide, 1-inch-deep mortises centered on each post.

3 Then cut ½-inch-wide, 1-inch-long tenons on both ends of each rail to fit the mortises in the

posts. The quickest way to do this is with a dado blade in the table saw. Use the miter gauge to guide the cut, and set the rip fence as a stop to define the shoulders of the tenon.

4 Once the tenons are cut, the next step is to cut a ¼-inch × ¼-inch groove on the *inside* edge of each rail for the slats; see the slat/groove detail on page 63. Since these grooves are offset and not centered on the rails, it's important to always keep the *outside* face of each rail against the rip fence as you cut the groove. Make sure to use a push block to make the cut and a featherboard to press the slat firmly against the rip fence.

5 Since the rail tenons will butt into each other inside the mortises, you'll need to miter the ends so the shoulders will butt up firmly against the posts. You can do this three ways: miter by hand with a chisel; trim them on the table saw with the blade angled to 45 degrees; or, as shown here, cut them with a power miter saw. It's a good idea to mark the angle on the end of each tenon to prevent a miscut.

6 Here again, you'll need to either round over the tenon or square up the mortise for the parts to fit together. It's quick and easy to round over the ends of the tenons with a sharp chisel or file.

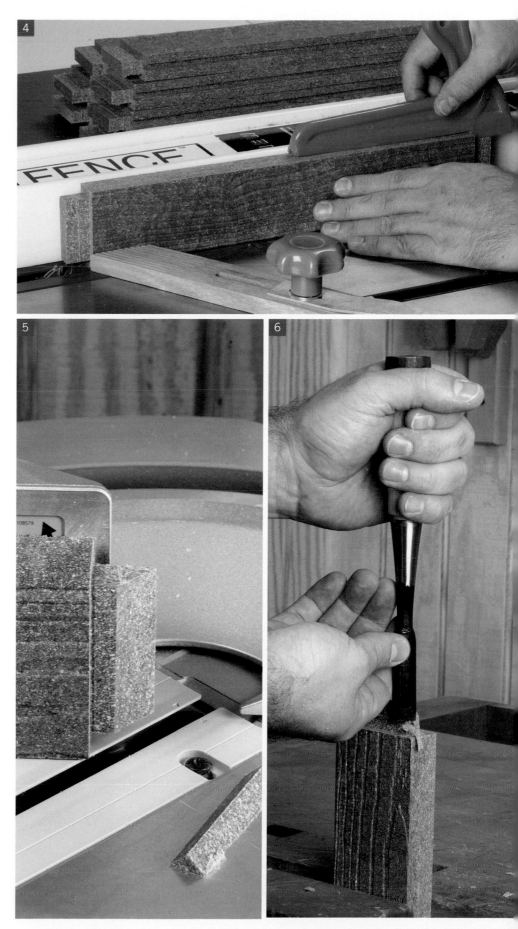

7 To make the slats (D, E, and F), first dry-assemble the planter stand and measure the distance between the rails. Then add ½ inch to this (the combined length of the tenons) and cut the vertical slats to length (they should be 11 inches long). Next, trim the narrow slats to width.

8 The slats fit into the grooves you cut in the rails earlier. Since the slats are ½ inch thick, you'll need to cut a ¼-inch × ¼-inch rabbet on the end of each slat to form a tongue to fit into the groove. You can cut the rabbet on the router table with a straight bit, or with a dado blade in the table saw as shown here. Use the miter gauge to guide the workpiece, and set the rip fence as a stop to define the shoulder of the rabbet.

9 Dry-assemble the planter stand with the slats to make sure everything fits. Then rout ⅛-inch chamfer on the long edges of the slats, on all long edges of the rails, and on the long edges of the posts. Rout a ¼-inch chamfer on the tops and bottoms of the posts.

10 To assemble the planter stand, start by gluing up two side assemblies (two posts, two rails, and the appropriate number of slats), using epoxy and clamps. Note: It's a good idea to apply a bead of silicone inside the grooves in the rails before inserting the slats, to keep them from sliding around.

11 After the epoxy cures, connect the two side assemblies with the remaining rails and slats, again using epoxy and clamps.

12 Finally, measure from slat to slat inside the planter and cut the bottom slats (G) to length. These should be a press fit and simply rest on the top edges of the lower rails. The real beauty of this project should be evident now—there's no finish required!

patio table

If you can saw a board and drive a screw, you can build this simple, attractive patio table in an afternoon. Fancy techniques? Not here—just solid construction.

- **Material:** Pine
- **Adhesive:** Titebond II
- **Finish:** 1 coat oil-based primer; 2 coats white satin enamel
- **Level:** Easy

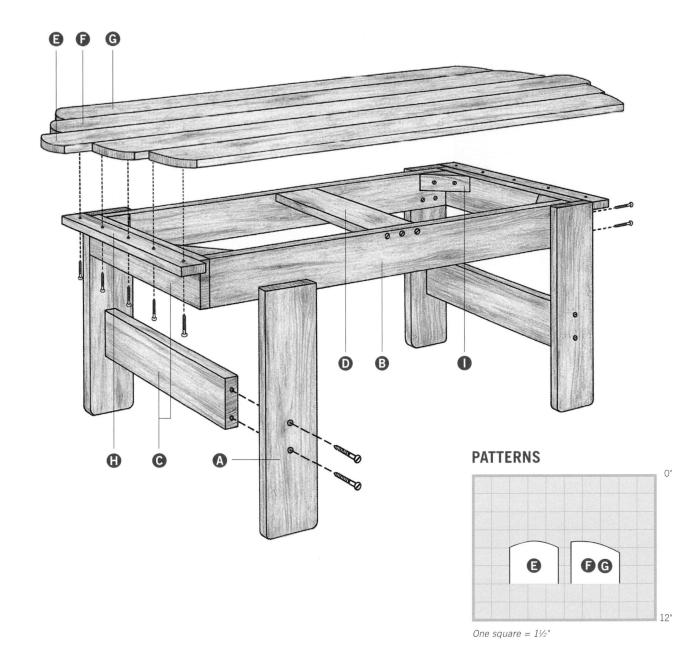

PATTERNS

0"

12"

One square = 1½"

Easy to build, pleasing, sturdy, and easy to customize to match your other patio furniture. What more could you want? Just alter the shape of the ends to complement the style of your existing pieces for a "suite" effect. You can leave the ends square to form a rectangular top, cut a gentle curve, or vary the lengths, as we did here to match the Adirondack chair shown on page 4.

MATERIALS LIST

PART	NAME	QUANTITY	DIMENSIONS
A	Legs	4	3½" × 16" – ¾" stock
B	Aprons	2	3½" × 30" – ¾" stock
C	Stretchers	4	3½" × 17" – ¾" stock
D	Brace	1	3½" × 15½" – ¾" stock
E	Middle slat	1	4" × 46" – ¾" stock
F	Side slats	2	4" × 42" – ¾" stock
G	End slats	2	4" × 38" – ¾" stock
H	Cleats	2	1¾" × 18½" – ¾" stock
I	Corner blocks	4	3½" × 3½" – 1½" stock

Assembly Instructions

The patio table is made up of two side assemblies that are connected with stretchers to form a frame. The top rests directly on the frame and is attached with corner blocks; see the illustration on page 69. To begin construction, start by cutting the pieces to length and width according to the materials list on page 69.

1 The two side assemblies are identical, and each is made up of two legs (A) and an apron (B). To prevent the bottoms of the legs from catching when the table is moved, lay out, cut, and sand a 1-inch radius on the bottom corner of each leg. To assemble the sides, position the pieces to form a U-shape as shown. Offset the legs so they overhang 1 inch past the ends of the apron, and use a try square make sure the leg is square to the apron. Then attach the apron to the legs with glue and #8 × 1¼-inch screws.

2 The two side assemblies are connected with four stretchers (C)—two at the top and two lower down on the legs—and a brace (D). Clamp a stretcher between each of the side assemblies at the top. The easiest way to do this is to position the side assemblies upside down on your work surface, as shown. The top stretchers butt up against the ends of the aprons. To secure them, drill pilot holes through the stretchers into the aprons and attach with #8 × 2-inch screws. Then screw the brace (D) centered between the rails so it's flush with the top of the aprons.

3 For the lower stretchers, flip the table upright and make a pair of 4½-inch long spacer blocks from scrap to position the lower stretchers, as shown. Center the stretcher on the legs, and lay out and drill two pilot holes in each leg. Then secure them to the legs with #8 × 2-inch screws.

4 All that's left is to add the top. It's made up of five slats (E, F, and G) that are held together underneath with a pair of cleats. The top is secured to the frame by way of four corner blocks. How you treat these slats will depend on the style you're after. For a rectangular or a gently curved top, cut them all the same length. Then for a curved top, use a bent stick to lay out a gentle curve and cut out and sand the curve on the ends. For the table shown here, it's best to make a pattern for the slats and use this to lay out the curve, as shown. (Patterns for the slats are shown on page 69.)

5 Once you've shaped the slats, they can be assembled by laying them face down on a table and inserting ¼-inch spacers between them. Then center the base upside down on the slats from end to end and from side to side. Position the cleats (H) on the ends so they butt up against the frame, and attach them to the slats with glue and #8 × 1¼-inch screws, one per slat, as shown.

6 Next, flip the frame right side up, drill holes for screws, and attach *corner blocks* (I) to the inside corners of the frame with glue and #8 × 1½-inch screws, as shown. To secure the top, place it face down on the work surface, position the frame on top, and screw through the corner blocks and into the top using #8 × 2-inch screws, as shown in 6b. Finally, sand the entire project with 150-grit sandpaper and apply the finish of your choice.

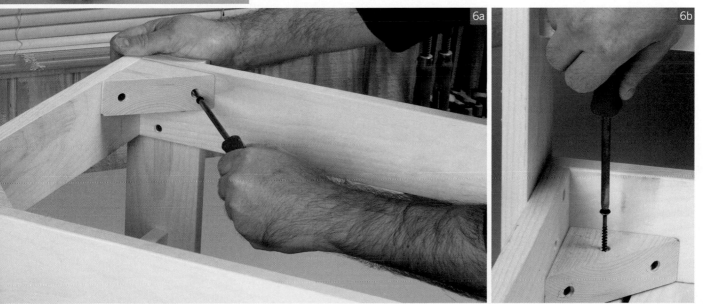

round dining table

No tablecloth, please, just place mats, so that everyone can appreciate the intricate slat pattern of this "look twice" table. Its sturdy, well-balanced form combines a square base with a round top—and terrific eye appeal.

- **Materials:** Redwood and cedar
- **Adhesive:** Resorcinol or Titebond II
- **Finish:** 3 coats of satin spar varnish
- **Level:** Challenging

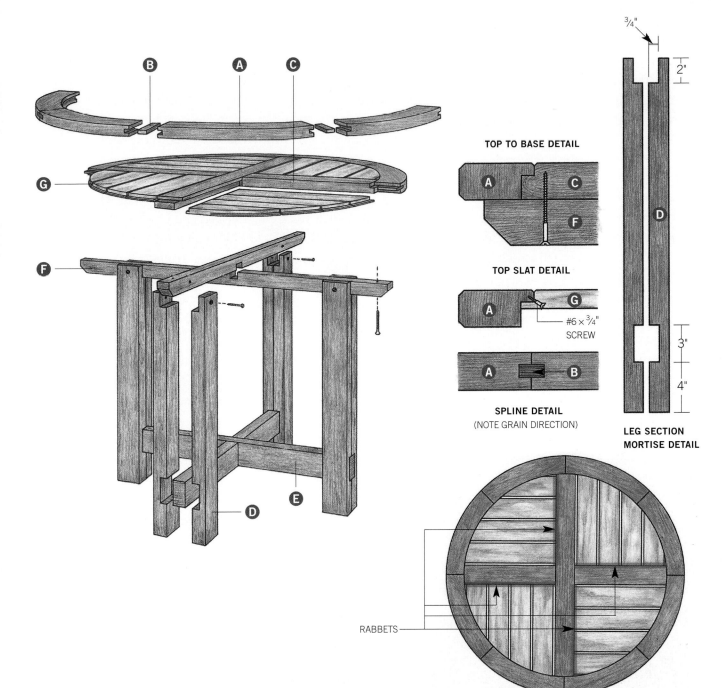

TOP TO BASE DETAIL

TOP SLAT DETAIL

#6 × 3/4"
SCREW

SPLINE DETAIL
(NOTE GRAIN DIRECTION)

**LEG SECTION
MORTISE DETAIL**

3/4"

2"

3"

4"

RABBETS

Brawn meets beauty in this deceptively simple-looking piece that presents a fair challenge. Notice the splines in the edge of the round frame; also, each slat is calibrated to match the curve. This is precision work that you'll want to accent by crafting the top frame and base in one wood, and choosing a contrasting wood for the slats. You'll be glad you took your time to build this "keeper."

MATERIALS LIST

PART	NAME	QUANTITY	DIMENSIONS
A	Top sides	8	5 1/2" × 18" – 1 1/2" stock
B	Splines	8	1" × 5 1/2" – 1/2" stock
C	Top cross bars	2	3" × 36 1/4" – 1 1/2" stock
D	Leg sections	8	3" × 28 1/2" – 1 1/2" stock
E	Rails	2	3" × 30" – 1 1/2" stock
F	Top braces	2	2" × 39" – 1 1/2" stock
G	Top slats*	16	3 1/2": 4 @ 18", 16", 14", and 11" – 3/4" stock
*Rough dimension, cut to fit			

Assembly Instructions

The round table features a top that rests on a base made up of four legs connected with rails and top braces. The top is a round frame that holds two crossbars and accepts a set of slats. To begin construction, cut the parts to width and length according to the materials list on page 73.

1 The frame for the top is made by joining eight mitered pieces together with splines, and then cutting this into a perfect round. To make the frame, cut the top side pieces (A) to a rough length of 19 inches. Then cut a 22½-degree miter on one end of each piece. Miter-cut the other end at 22½ degrees, using a long fence attached to the miter gauge and a stop block clamped to the fence to set a finished length of 18 inches. Note: It's a good idea to cut eight test pieces from scrap plywood first—being off just a fraction of a degree can produce gaps.

2 Next, cut a ½-inch-wide groove centered on the thickness on both ends of each top side. Then cut ½-inch-thick splines (B) 1 inch wide to fit the grooves, as described in step 2 on page 46 and step 4 on page 47, respectively. Now you can assemble the top side pieces with glue and splines. Place the parts on a half sheet of plywood protected by a drop cloth, and use a band clamp to snug up the joints.

3 Temporarily attach the glued-up frame to the half sheet of plywood with double-sided tape *with the good side down*. Also tape

a square scrap of 1½-inch-thick wood to the center of the frame. Find the exact center of the frame and drill a pilot hole in the small scrap for a panhead screw. Attach the circle jig to the scrap block and cut a circle, taking a series of light passes—about ¼ inch at a time until you've cut all the way through and just into the plywood. Then move the jig to the other hole you drilled in it, and cut the inside of the circle to create a 3-inch-wide frame.

4 Remove the frame from the half sheet of plywood. If necessary, drizzle lacquer thinner between the frame and the plywood to loosen the tape's adhesive. Then rout a ½-inch-wide rabbet with a rabbeting bit around the *inside* perimeter of the frame to accept the cross bars and slats. Take a series of light cuts, lowering the bit each time until you're left with a ½-inch-thick ledge.

5 Cut the cross bars (C) to length to fit inside the rabbeted edges of the top. Then cut ¾-inch-deep, 3-inch-wide half-laps centered on each piece. Next, rout a ½-inch-wide rabbet on the end of each piece so the faces of the cross bars are flush with the face of the frame. Next, attach the cross bars to the underside of the top with screws. Drill countersunk pilot holes at an angle and drive in #6 × 1¼-inch screws. Finally, rout a ⅛-inch chamfer around the inside edges of the frame and cross bars.

Circle-Routing Jig

The simplest way to cut a perfectly round circle is to rout it with a jig made from a piece of ¼-inch hardboard. Cut the strip to match the width of your router base and about 24 inches long. Remove your router's base and use it as a template to mark mounting hole locations on the hardboard. Then attach the router and insert a straight bit. Next, measure 21⅜ inches from the *inside* edge of the straight bit and mark and drill a hole (for a panhead screw) centered on the end of the jig. Finally, measure 17⅞ inches from the bit and drill another hole (for the inside of the frame).

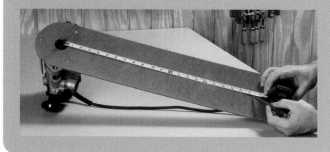

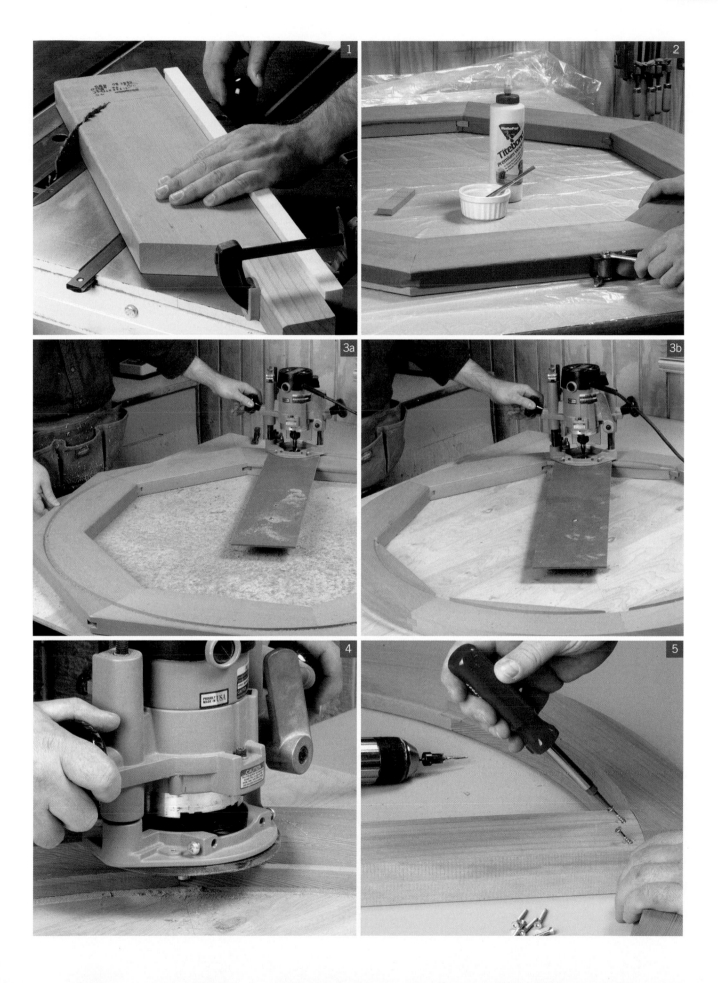

6 Each leg is made up of two 2 × 4 leg sections (D) that are notched and then glued together to create mortises for the rails and top braces. Cut ¾-inch-deep dadoes and rabbets at the locations shown in the detail drawing on page 73. Then assemble each leg section in pairs with glue and clamps, making sure the dadoes and rabbets align. It's a good idea to protect softwood from the jaws of the clamps with scraps of wood. Next, cut ¼ inch off each face of the glued-up legs to create 3-inch-square sections. To complete the legs, rout a ⅛-inch chamfer on the long edges of each leg and a ¼-inch chamfer on the bottom of each leg.

7 Both the rails (E) and the top braces (F) are joined in the middle with half-laps. Cut centered, 1½-inch-wide half-laps in each piece: 1½ inches deep for the rails and 1 inch deep for the top braces. Use the miter gauge to guide the workpiece, and set the rip fence to define the shoulders of the dadoes. Next, to "hide" the top braces, cut a 1-inch-wide chamfer on the bottom end of each brace.

8 Assemble the base by first gluing the rail half-laps together and then attaching the legs with glue. Then glue the half-laps of the top braces together and insert this in the top of the base. Drill countersunk pilot holes, and attach the top braces to the legs with #8 × 2½-inch screws.

9 All that's left is to add the top slats (G). Although this isn't difficult, it is rather tedious since each slat must be cut to match the curve of the top, and then the ends rabbeted to fit into the frame. Start by placing the top upside down on your work surface. Then rout ½-inch-wide rabbets on the designated cross bars to create a ½-inch-thick ledge to accept the slats (see the detail drawings on page 73).

10 Next, cut the 3½-inch-wide slats to rough length. Slip sets of slats under the top so one end of each slat extends ½ inch past the rabbeted edge of a cross bar. Adjust the slats for an even gap, and then trace around the inside edge of the frame to transfer the arc to the slats. Number the slats before you remove them. Cut the curves to shape, and sand the edges smooth. Then rout a ½-inch-wide, ½-inch-deep rabbet on both ends of each slat, and rout a ⅛-inch chamfer on all top edges of each slat. Finally, slip the slats into the frame and secure them to the frame with #6 × ¾-inch screws driven in at an angle.

11 Position the base on the top so the top braces align with the cross bars and the base is centered. Then drill countersunk pilot holes through the top braces and just into the top for screws. Attach the base to the top with #8 × 3-inch screws.

folding picnic table

Here's a handsome twist on a ho-hum standard. Its elegant lines and roomy surface offer bonus convenience. After the haute cuisine or hot dogs, just fold it up and slip it into a narrow space.

- **Material: Mahogany**
- **Adhesive: Resorcinol or Titebond II**
- **Finish: 2 coats of satin exterior polyurethane**
- **Level: Moderate**

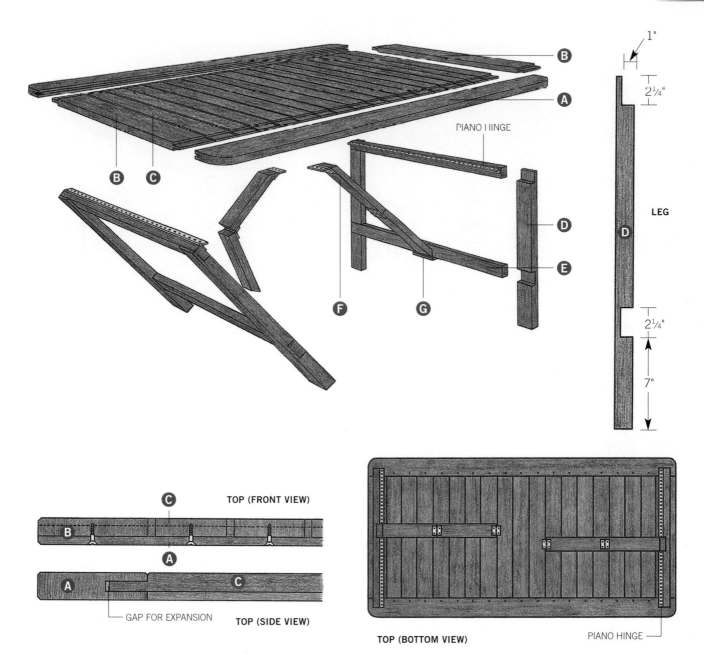

1"

2¼"

LEG

D

2¼"

7"

PIANO HINGE

B

A

B C

D

E

F G

TOP (FRONT VIEW)

C

B

A

TOP (SIDE VIEW)

A

C

GAP FOR EXPANSION

TOP (BOTTOM VIEW)

PIANO HINGE

Tired of the same old 2 × 4 picnic table? Want something a little more polished? Build this fine, functional piece and enjoy its form for years. Even though it folds up for easy storage, this multi-slatted model is far from flimsy. It calls on full-length piano hinges and sturdy braces to stand up to meals, weather, whatever your outdoor situation dishes out. When others ask where you bought it, smile modestly.

MATERIALS LIST

PART	NAME	QUANTITY	DIMENSIONS
A	Top front/back	2	4" × 59" – ⁵⁄₄ stock
B	Top sides	2	4" × 30" – ⁵⁄₄ stock
C	Top slats	17	2⁵⁄₈" × 29¾" – ¾" stock
D	Legs	4	2¼" × 27" – 1³⁄₈ stock
E	Rails	4	2¼" × 30" – ⁵⁄₄ stock
F	Braces	4	3" × 13" – ⁵⁄₄ stock
G	Stops	2	1¼" × 3" – ³⁄₈ stock

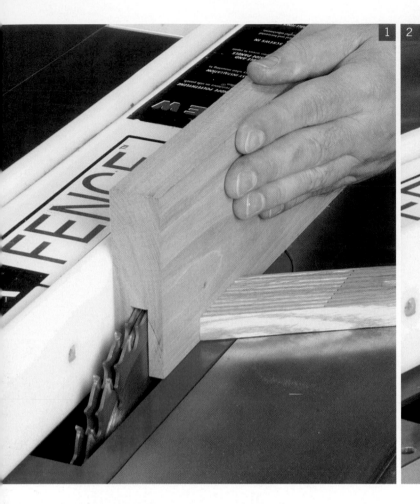

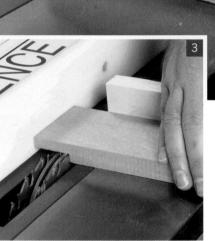

Assembly Instructions

The folding picnic table consists of a top, two leg units, and a set of braces to hold the legs in the open position (see the top illustration on page 79). The top is basically a frame that accepts a set of slats. Start construction by cutting the parts to width and length according to the materials list.

1 The top frame is made up of a front and back (A) and two sides (B), joined with a tongue-and-groove joint. Tongues are cut on the sides and grooves are cut in the front and back. Instead of cutting stopped grooves near the ends of the front and back, you'll cut the grooves the full length to accept the top slats (C). Cut a $\frac{3}{8}$-inch-wide groove ($1\frac{1}{2}$ inches deep) centered on the *inside* edges of the front and back with a dado blade on the table saw.

2 Next, cut $\frac{3}{8}$-inch-thick, $1\frac{1}{2}$-inch-long tenons (tongues) on the ends of the top sides to fit the grooves. Use the miter gauge to guide the piece, and position the rip fence as a stop to define the tenon length. To soften the corners of the table, lay out a $2\frac{1}{2}$-inch radius on the ends of the front and back; cut these to shape and sand them smooth. Dry-assemble the frame parts and rout a $\frac{1}{8}$-inch chamfer on the *inside* top edges of the frame and

outside bottom edges of the frame; rout a $\frac{1}{4}$-inch chamfer on the outside top edges of the frame.

3 For the $\frac{3}{4}$-inch-thick slats to fit into the grooves, rabbets are cut on the ends to create tongues. Cut the rabbets $1\frac{3}{8}$ inches long to leave a $\frac{1}{8}$-inch gap to allow the wood to expand and contract. Use the miter gauge to guide the slat, and set the rip fence as a stop to define the length of the rabbet.

4 To complete the slats, rout a
⅛-inch chamfer on all top
edges of the slats. You can do
this with a chamfering bit, but
to rout the top of the rabbeted
end, you'll likely need to remove
the bearing on the router bit
and use your router table fence
as shown in the top photo.
Alternately, you could sand this
chamfer by hand or use a 45-
degree veining bit since it has no
bearing—but without a bearing
to guide the bit, the fence must
be used for routing all the edges.

5 Now you can assemble the
top. Slip the slats into the
grooves in the front and back and
slide in the sides. Apply glue *only*
to the tongue-and-groove joint
on the ends of the top frame
pieces—*not* to the slats. The slats
are secured with screws next; this
lets them expand and contract
with changes in the weather.

6 Slide the slats back and forth
in the grooves in the front
and back until they're equally
spaced (about ⅜-inch gaps). Then
drill a countersunk hole through
the underside at each slat, centered
on the length of the groove and
into the slat. Secure the end of
each slat with a #6 × 1-inch screw.

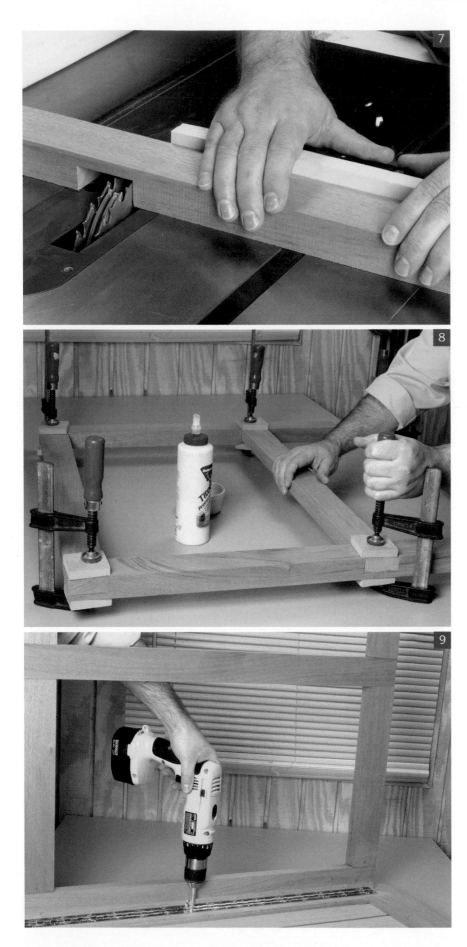

7 With the top complete, you can turn your attention to the leg units. Each is made up of two legs (D) and two rails (E). The rails fit in notches cut into the legs. Cut a 2¼-inch-wide, 1-inch-deep rabbet on the end of each leg and a 2¼-inch-wide, 1-inch-deep dado 7 inches up from the bottom of each leg (see the detail on page 79). Use the miter gauge to guide the leg, and set the rip fence to define the shoulders of the dado and rabbet.

8 Once the rabbets and dadoes have been cut, assemble the legs with glue and clamps. Make sure the legs glue up square by measuring diagonally across both corners. The measurements should be the same if the assembly is square; adjust as necessary. After the glue dries, rout a ⅛-inch chamfer on all edges and rout a ¼-inch chamfer on the bottom of each leg.

9 The leg units attach to the top with piano hinges. Begin by cutting a pair of 1½-inch-wide hinges to a length of 30 inches with a hacksaw, and file the cut ends smooth. The simplest way to attach the hinges is to first attach one hinge flap flush to the top inside of each leg. A self-centering bit (often referred to by the brand name—Vix bit) makes drilling these holes a snap. Then position a leg unit 1 inch in from the top side (B) and centered from side to side, and drill and screw it to the top. Repeat for the other side.

10 The only thing left to do is add the braces (F) and stops (G) that lock the legs in the open position. Cut a 55-degree angle on the ends of one pair of braces and a 35-degree miter on the other pair. Connect one 35-degree cut end to a 55-degree cut end with 2-inch brass hinges. Hinging the brace lets you snap them in place to lock the legs open.

11 One end of each brace attaches to the underside of the top with a 2-inch-wide hinge. The other end fits under a stop (G) that's screwed to the underside of the bottom rail of each leg unit. Note that the stops and braces are offset to allow the braces to fold up next to each other (see the detail drawing on page 79). Attach the stops so they protrude toward the *inside* of the top to create a lip to catch each brace.

12 To hinge the brace to the table top, first attach one hinge flap to the face of the 35-degree mitered end; then position the opposite end under the stop. Shift the brace as necessary so the hinged end rests flat on the table top. Mark hole positions for the hinge and drill pilot holes; attach with screws. Sand the entire project with 150-grit sandpaper and apply the finish of your choice. Note: You'll find it easier if you remove the legs for finishing.

folding snack tray

Remember the old folding TV trays? Whether you do or not, you'll appreciate the convenience of this use-it-and-stash-it snack table. Simple and quick to build, it'll suit everything from parties to, yes, watching TV.

- **Material:** Mahogany
- **Adhesive:** Titebond II
- **Finish:** 2 coats of exterior satin polyurethane
- **Level:** Easy

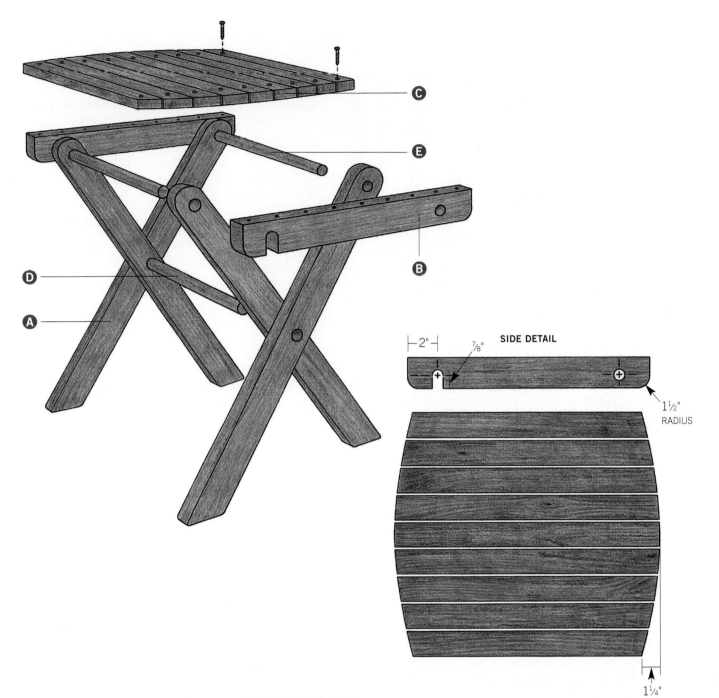

SIDE DETAIL

2"

7/8"

1½" RADIUS

1¼"

Got a free afternoon and some hand tools? Then get going on this handy folding tray, and you'll have it done for tonight's relaxation. It's customizable, too: You can choose to leave the top slats square, or cut a gentle curve to complement other outdoor pieces. One note for appearance's sake: Use dowels of the same type of wood you're using to build the table top.

MATERIALS LIST

PART	NAME	QUANTITY	DIMENSIONS
A	Legs	4	2" × 24" – ⁵⁄₄ stock
B	Sides	2	2" × 16" – ³⁄₄" stock
C	Slats	9	1⁵⁄₈" × 17½ – ³⁄₄" stock
D	Middle rung	1	13" – ³⁄₄" dowel
E	Top rungs	2	14½" – ³⁄₄" dowel

Assembly Instructions

The folding snack tray consists of pairs of legs connected by dowels to form an "X" in use. The legs connect to the top via a pair of sides (see the top illustration on page 85). The top is just a set of slats that are screwed to the sides. To begin construction, cut the parts to width and length according to the materials list.

1 Start work on the legs (A) by laying out centered, ¾-inch-diameter holes for the dowels that connect them: one hole at the midpoint of the leg, the other hole 1 inch down from the top. Clamp pairs of legs together and drill holes through both legs at once.

2 Miter the bottom end of each leg by making a 30-degree angled cut. You can do this by hand with a back saw, on the table saw, or as shown here, with a miter saw.

3 In order for the legs to be able to pivot once they're attached to the sides, the tops of the legs need to be rounded over. Lay out a 1-inch radius on the top of each leg. Then cut them to shape and sand the ends smooth. To complete the legs, rout a ¼-inch round-over on all edges.

4 The next step is to make the sides (B). Start by laying out and drilling holes for the top rungs 2 inches in from the ends and ⅞ inch up from the bottom edge. To create a notch on one end of the side to slip over a top rung, scribe a line from the outside edge of the hole to the bottom edge of the side.

5 Saw out the waste. Next, lay out, cut, and sand a 1½-inch radius on the bottom corners of the sides (see the detail on page 85). Finally, rout a ¼-inch round-over on the *bottom* edges of the sides and around the inside edges of the notch.

6 To make the top, first clamp the slats (C) together with ⅛-inch-thick spacers in between; number them for easy reassembly. Then use a bar clamp and a thin strip of wood to create a gentle curve (or leave square if you prefer). Trace around the strip with a pencil, remove the clamps, and then cut curves on each slat. Sand the edges smooth. When you're finished sanding, rout a ¼-inch round-over on all slat edges.

7 Now you can assemble the tray. First cut a 12⅞-inch-wide square scrap of wood, and clamp this between the sides to hold them in position for attaching the slats. Then reassemble the slats on top of the sides with spacers. Clamp them together temporarily so the slats are centered from back to front and from side to side. Next, lay out and drill countersunk pilot holes centered on the thickness of the sides and the width of the slats. Secure the slats with #8 × 1½-inch screws. Finally, drill holes for ¼-inch dowels and use these to pin the middle rung (D) to one set of legs. Likewise, pin one top rung (E) to the legs on the notch side and pin the sides to the other top rung on the opposite side.

tile table

Elegant lines, classic construction, and plenty of room for the entire family—what more could you want in an outdoor table? Ready for a new look? Just replace the lift-out tiles.

- **Material:** White oak
- **Adhesive:** Resorcinol
- **Finish:** 3 coats of satin spar varnish
- **Level:** Challenging

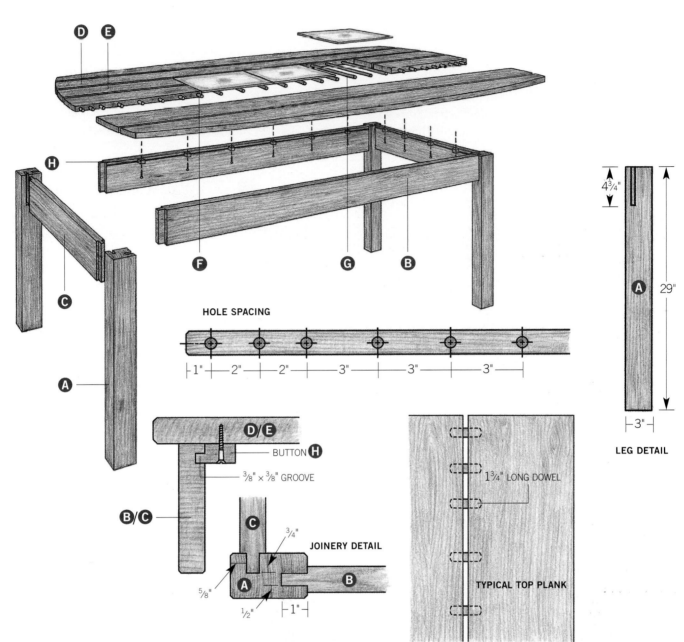

HOLE SPACING

1" — 2" — 2" — 3" — 3" — 3"

LEG DETAIL

4¾" 29" 3"

BUTTON Ⓗ

⅜" × ⅜" GROOVE

D/E

B/C

JOINERY DETAIL

¾"

⅝"

½" 1"

1¾" LONG DOWEL

TYPICAL TOP PLANK

What a super design for an outdoor table! The replaceable tile top holds hot serving pieces, while the planks adjust for wood movement. The tabletop planks are joined with dowels that leave a gap between each piece for drainage; this also lets the wood expand and contract, without splitting or cracking. The top attaches to the base with wood "buttons" that also help prevent damage. (For more on these, see page 93.)

MATERIALS LIST

PART	NAME	QUANTITY	DIMENSIONS
A	Legs	4	3" × 29" – 1¾" stock
B	Front/back aprons	2	5" × 56" – 5/4 stock
C	Side aprons	2	5" × 28" – 5/4 stock
D	Long top planks	4	6" × 72" – 5/4 stock
E	Short top planks	4	6" × 18" – 5/4 stock
F	Short dowels	92	1¾" × ½" dowels
G	Long dowels	11	14⅛" × ½" dowels
H	Buttons	20	1" × 1½" – ¾" stock

Assembly Instructions

The tile dining table features a top made of a set of planks joined together with short dowels (see the top illustration on page 89). Longer dowels span a section in the center to support 12-inch-square ceramic tiles. The top rests on a base made up of four legs and front, back, and side aprons. To begin construction, cut the parts to width and length according to the materials list.

1 The legs (A) are joined to the aprons with open-ended mortise-and-tenon joints. The first step is to rout ½-inch-wide stopped grooves (the mortises) 4¾ inches down on two adjacent faces of each leg (see the detail drawing on page 89). You're making two sets of bookmatched legs here. Clamp a scrap block on the router table fence to serve as a stop, and rout the first groove.

2 Then reposition the fence and cut a stopped groove on the adjacent face. Next, rout a ⅛-inch chamfer along the long edges of each leg and a ¼-inch chamfer on the bottom of each leg.

3 Now you can cut tenons on the ends of front, back, and side aprons (B, C) to fit the grooves (mortises) you cut in the legs. Use a dado blade in the table saw and guide the workpiece with the miter gauge. Position the rip fence to serve as a stop to define the shoulders. You'll cut three shoulders: one on each face and one on the bottom edge.

4 The next step is either to square up the bottom of each groove in the legs or to round over the bottom of the tenons on the ends of the aprons as shown here.

5 The top attaches to the base by way of "buttons" (see page 93) that fit in grooves cut near the top inside face of each apron. This groove is ⅜ inch wide and ⅜ inch deep and is ⅜ inch down from the top edge. You can cut this three ways: with a straight bit with a portable router and an edge guide; with a table-mounted router; or with a dado blade in the table saw as shown here.

6 To assemble the base, first dry, fit and clamp the parts to make sure everything fits. If everything does, apply glue to the tenons of one side apron and clamp this between a pair of the legs; repeat for the other end. Then apply glue to the tenons of the front and back aprons and clamp these between the two end assemblies. Measure diagonally from corner to corner and compare the measurements. If they're the same, the base is square. If not, apply a clamp from corner to corner and apply pressure to "rack" the base until the diagonal measurements match.

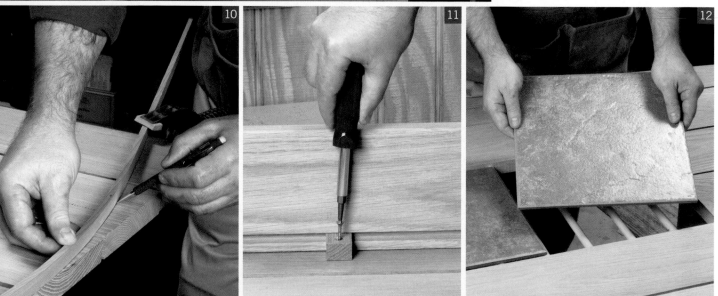

7 With the base complete, you can start on the top. Begin by laying out the hole locations on the edges of the long and short planks (D, E) for the dowels that connect the planks. The most accurate way to do this is to clamp the planks together with the ends flush, and lay out the holes all at once (see the detail drawing on page 89 for locations). Make sure to label the tops of the planks and their order.

8 Once the holes are laid out, drill ½-inch holes, ¾ inch deep at each location. Use a high fence on the drill press or a doweling jig for this—depth is critical. Then cut short dowels (F) to a length of 1¾ inches. A precise way to do this is to drill a hole slightly larger than ½ inch in a scrap of wood to an exact depth of 1¾ inches. Then slip a dowel rod into the hole and adjust the rip fence, or clamp a straightedge to the band saw table to cut the dowel flush with the edge. Remove the short dowel, insert the dowel rod and repeat. To make it easier to insert the dowels in the planks, sand chamfers on both ends.

9 Now you can assemble the top, starting with pairs of long planks—use clamps as necessary, continuing until the top is assembled. Use a slow-setting glue, as this assembly process will take some time.

10 Now measure in 2½ inches from each corner and bend a thin stick to create a gradual curve on both ends and sides. Cut the shape with a saber saw, and sand the edges smooth—a belt sander on edge works well for this. Then rout a ³⁄₁₆-inch chamfer on the top edge and a ⅛-inch chamfer on the bottom edge.

11 To attach the top to the base, first place the top upside down on a padded work surface and center the base on it from side to side and from front to back. Secure the base to the top with buttons and #8 × 1½-inch screws (see Buttons at right). Place a button on the width of each plank and about every 6 inches– 8 inches along the length of the long planks.

12 Then flip the assembled table right side up and set the tiles on top of the long dowels. The tiles shown here are 12-inch-square ceramic floor tiles.

Buttons

Wood buttons are a great way to attach a table top to its base. The buttons fit into grooves cut in the aprons and not only hold the top securely in place, but also slide within the grooves as the planks expand and contract, reacting to changing weather conditions. Making buttons is a four-step process.

1. Start by cutting a ³⁄₈-inch × ³⁄₈-inch rabbet on the *width* of a piece of ¾-inch-thick stock.

2. Then cut the rabbeted end to a width of 1½ inches to create a strip.

3. Next, cut the strip into 1-inch-wide pieces. Clamp a stop block on the rip fence about 3 inches back from the front edge of the blade, and adjust the rip fence so when the strip is butted up against the stop block, you'll end up with a 1-inch-wide button. Use the miter gauge to guide the strip past the blade.

4. Finally, drill a countersunk pilot hole in the underside of each button, centered on the body, for the mounting screw.

doghouse

If dogs could build, this is how doghouses would look. Although not elegant, it's a pooch palace: It has a separate entrance and a private room, and it's insulated. Plus, it's custom-sized to fit the pup.

- **Materials:** 2 × 4 cedar, T1-11 siding, plywood, exterior plywood, shingles, foam insulation
- **Adhesive:** Construction adhesive
- **Finish:** 2 coats of exterior paint
- **Level:** Moderate

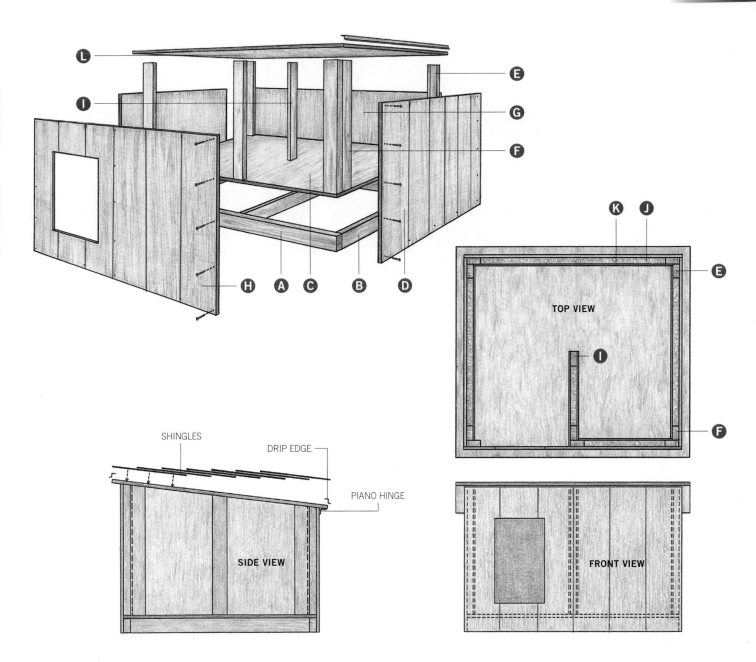

SHINGLES

DRIP EDGE

PIANO HINGE

SIDE VIEW

TOP VIEW

FRONT VIEW

This project is based on the American Humane Society's recommended doghouse design. Whether your dog stays outside all the time or only once in a while, it deserves a house that fits. The doghouse should be wide enough to turn around in and long enough to stretch out. Don't over-build: The dog's body heat warms the house. If it's too spacious, he'll be cold. Equally important is the partition wall near the door which acts as a wind/rain break.

MATERIALS LIST

PART	NAME	QUANTITY	DIMENSIONS
A	Base front/back	2	2 × 4 – cedar
B	Base sides/divider	3	2 × 4 – cedar
C	Base top	1	¾"-thick exterior-rated plywood
D	Sides	2	T1-11 or other exterior-rated siding
E	Back studs	4	2 × 4 – cedar
F	Front studs	6	2 × 4 – cedar
G	Back	1	T1-11 or other exterior-rated siding
H	Front	1	T1-11 or other exterior-rated siding
I	Partition stud	1	2 × 4 – cedar
J	Insulation	5	1½"-thick rigid foam
K	Interior panels	6	¼" plywood
L	Roof	1	¾"-thick exterior-rated plywood

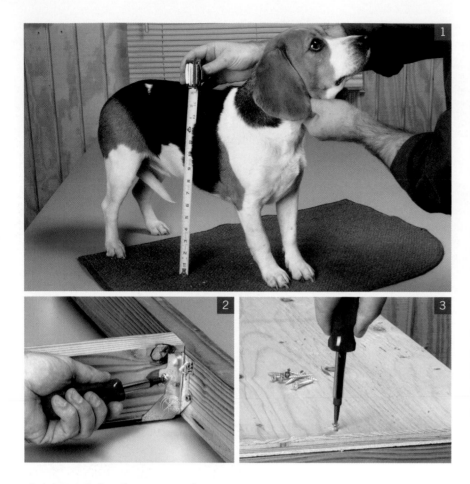

Assembly Instructions

The doghouse is made up of a 2 × 4 base with a plywood top that's surrounded by T1-11 walls. Corner framing inside the walls helps create a strong structure and allows you to add rigid foam insulation and the inner walls. The roof hinges onto the back and lifts up for easy cleaning (see the illustrations on page 95). To begin, start by measuring your pup to determine the size of the project parts (see step 1 below). Then cut the parts to width and length per your calculations.

1 The general rule of thumb for sizing a doghouse is to make the width of the house equal to the dog's length plus 12 inches, and the length of the house equal to the dog's length plus 18 inches. The height should equal the dog's height plus 9 inches in the front and slope back to the dog's height plus 3 inches. Measure the height, width, and length of your dog and determine the size of the parts.

2 Attach the parts of the base—front/back (A) and sides and divider (B)—with joist hangers and brackets using galvanized screws.

3 Then cut a base top (C) from ³⁄₄-inch-thick exterior plywood to cover the base. Drill countersunk holes and secure the top with 1¹⁄₂-inch galvanized screws.

4 Lay out and cut a pair of bookmatched sides (D) from ⁵⁄₈-inch-thick T1-11 or exterior plywood. Cut the angle on top by clamping a straightedge to the plywood to serve as a guide for a circular saw. An easy way to support the cut without damaging your work surface is to slip a piece of rigid foam under the plywood; then set your saw to just cut through the plywood.

5 Now you can attach the sides to the base. Position each side so it's flush with the ends of the base and flush with the bottom. Then drill countersunk pilot holes and secure it to the base with 1¹⁄₂-inch galvanized screws.

6 Each corner of the doghouse has a pair of studs screwed together to form a brace. Because the sides are angled, you'll need to angle one end of each stud. Start by cutting four back studs (E) slightly longer than the back side. Cut six front studs (F) slightly longer than the front side. Then hold a stud flat against one end of the side and mark the angle directly on the stud with a pencil. Cut this angle, and also cut a matching angle on the top of the stud that attaches to this to form the corner. Screw the studs together with 3¹⁄₂-inch deck screws to make bookmatched pairs. Then attach the studs to the sides with 1¹⁄₂-inch galvanized screws. Repeat this for the front studs. You'll make three sets: two for the sides and one for the partition wall added later.

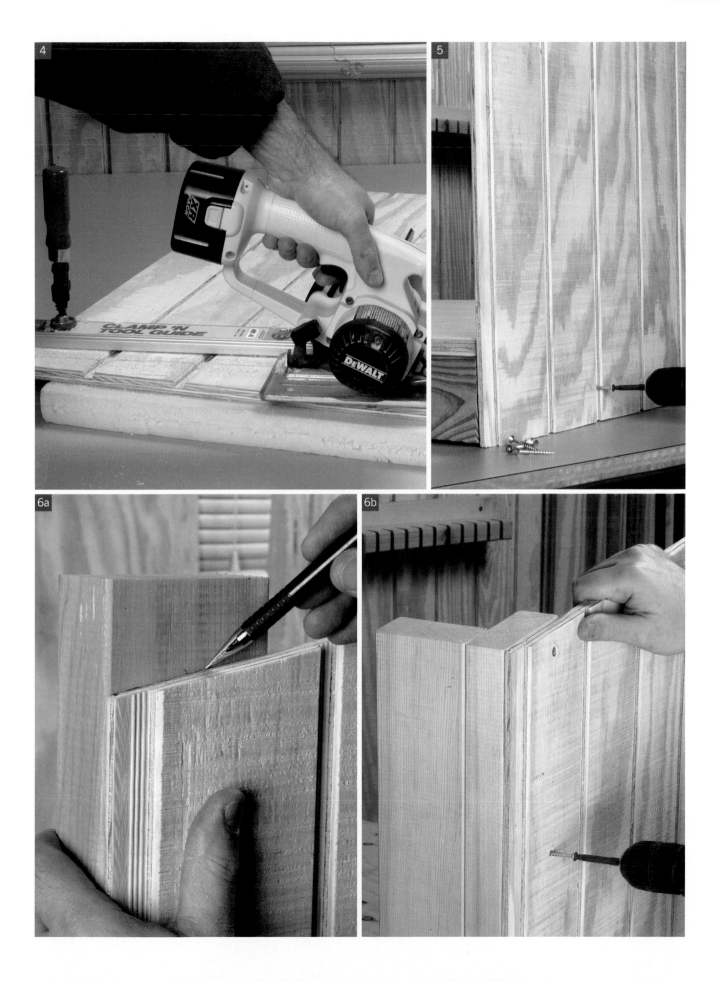

7 Now you can lay out, cut, and attach the back (G). Note that the top edge is beveled to match the angle of the sides. Next, lay out and cut the front (H) to size. Here again, the top edge will need to be beveled to match the angle of the sides. Before you attach the front, lay out the door opening. The opening should be as tall as the pup and his/her width plus 3 inches. Offset the opening 1½ inches up from the base top (C). Drill starter holes in the corners and cut the opening with a saber saw. Sand the edges smooth, and then attach the front.

8 The partition wall serves to keep the dog warm and dry as well as offering privacy (which means security, to a dog). Attach the remaining front stud pair to the front (H), set in 6 inches from the right side of the door opening. Then lay out a partition stud (I), centered on the depth of the doghouse. To determine the top angle for this piece, use a scrap of wood to span the sides at the midway point. Then place a straightedge on the back and rest it on the scrap. Butt the partition stud up against the straightedge and trace the angle directly on the stud. Miter the top and secure the bottom of the stud to the top base with screws. Then cut a panel (angled on top) from ¼-inch plywood to create the partition wall, and attach it to the front and partition stud with brads or staples.

9 To keep the pup warm, line the interior walls with 1½-inch-thick rigid foam insulation (J). Cut the pieces to size with a utility knife and attach them to the walls with construction adhesive.

10 Continue working on the interior walls by cutting ¼-inch interior panels (K) to fit in between the studs, nailing them in place. Although it might be tempting to skip this step, it's important to close off the insulation, which many dogs regard as a tasty treat.

11 The roof (L) attaches to the back of the doghouse via a piano hinge. Cut the roof to size so that there's a 1-inch overhang all the way around. Then cut a 1½-inch-wide piano hinge to match the length of the back (G); attach one hinge flap to the bottom, back edge of the roof, and the other to the back top edge of the back panel.

12 Attach the roofing of your choice. You can use asphalt shingles, or cedar shingles as shown here. Before you do this, protect the plywood edges by installing drip edge. (Alternately, you can dress up the doghouse by adding trim to the roof edges, around the door opening, and even adding a faux window.) Install a starter row of shingles and shingle the roof. Make sure to use ¾-inch nails so they don't poke through.

13 Brush on a couple of coats of exterior paint. If you added trim, paint it a different color. When you place the doghouse, slip a layer of 6-mil plastic underneath to serve as a vapor barrier to prevent moisture from rising up into the interior. Then lift up the roof and drop in a carpet remnant, followed by a puppy cushion. Add the dog's favorite chew toy and watch him enjoy his home away from home.

window box

You don't have to root yourself in the shop to make this simple yet impressive window accent. It looks like a custom piece, but builds easily. Practice saying "thank you" for the compliments to come.

- **Material:** Teak
- **Adhesive:** Epoxy
- **Finish:** Teak oil
- **Level:** Easy

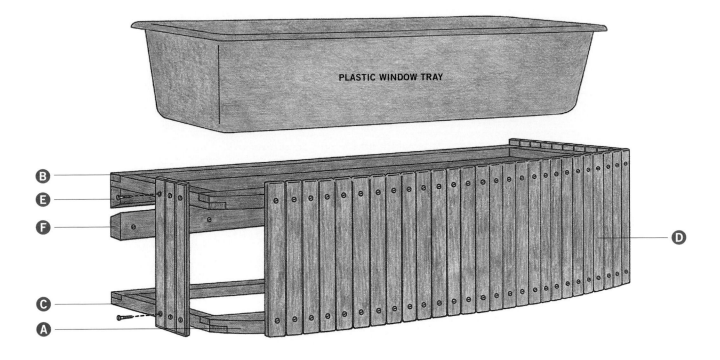

PLASTIC WINDOW TRAY

B
E
F
C
A
D

1/16" GAP
BETWEEN SLATS

B
C
CURVE DETAIL
A
3/4"

C
B

E
F

HANGER DETAIL

SLAT DETAIL

HALF-LAP DETAIL

s practical as it is attractive, this planter box will seem to "float" in front of your window. The secret? A hidden mounting system that keeps your greenery the center of attention. Another plus: The unit can be removed for cleaning, or off-season storage. Novice-level skills are welcome here to create the clean, custom-looking lines. Enhance any window with this, and a standard-sized plastic tray.

MATERIALS LIST

PART	NAME	QUANTITY	DIMENSIONS
A	Frame fronts	2	3" × 24 1/2" – 3/4" stock
B	Frame backs	2	3/4" × 24 1/2" – 3/4" stock
C	Frame sides	4	3/4" × 10 1/4" – 3/4" stock
D	Slats	50	3/4" × 7" – 1/4" stock
E	Cleat top	1	1 1/2" × 24 1/4" – 3/4" stock
F	Cleat bottom	1	1 1/2" × 24 1/4" – 3/4" stock

Assembly Instructions

The window box consists of a pair of frames with curved fronts that are spanned by a series of narrow, vertical slats. The box attaches to the house with a unique double-beveled cleat system (see the top illustration on page 101). The opening in each frame is 6½ inches wide by 23 inches long to fit a standard plastic tray. To begin, cut the frame parts to width and length according to the materials list.

1 To connect the parts of the frame together (A, B, and C), cut ⅜-inch-deep by ¾-inch-wide half-laps on the ends of the frame parts. You can do this by hand with a backsaw, on the table saw with a dado blade, or on the router table with a straight bit as shown here. If you rout the half-laps, make sure to back up the cut by clamping a scrap block to the frame part to prevent chipout.

2 After the half-laps have been cut, glue the frames together with epoxy and apply clamps at the joints to press the parts firmly together.

3 All that's left to do on the frames is to lay out and cut curves on the fronts. The simplest way to do this is to bend a thin strip of wood in a graceful curve and hold it in place with clamps. Then trace along the strip with a pencil. Since the curves on both frames must match, it's best to lay out one curve and use this to cut both frames. Temporarily fasten both frames together with double-sided tape, and then cut the curve on both frames at the same time on the band saw. Leave the frames taped together, and sand the curve smooth with a drum sander.

4 With the frames complete, you can turn your attention to the slats (D). The only challenge is safely cutting the thin strips you'll need for these. An easy way to do this is to make a jig for the

table saw. The jig is nothing more than a scrap of plywood with a thin cleat attached at the end. This cleat forms a lip that's used to guide the wood safely past the saw blade. By setting the rip fence to the width of the jig plus $\frac{1}{4}$ inch, every strip will be exactly $\frac{1}{4}$ inch thick. After you've cut sufficient strips to width, trim them to a length of 7 inches. Then drill countersunk holes for screws centered on each slat and $\frac{3}{4}$ inch in from both ends. Finally, rout or sand a $\frac{1}{8}$-inch chamfer on all front edges of each slat.

5 To assemble the window box, first cut a pair of $4\frac{3}{4}$-inch-wide scrap-wood spacers and clamp these between the frames. Then begin attaching slats on the ends. Position a slat so it extends an equal amount past the frames, and drill countersunk pilot holes. Then secure the slat with #6 × $\frac{3}{4}$-inch screws. Use a strip of plastic laminate as a spacer to create uniform gaps between the slats. Repeat this for the front slats.

6 Next, make the top and bottom cleats (E, F) that form the hanging system. You can cut both of these from a single $2\frac{1}{2}$-inch-wide, $24\frac{1}{4}$-inch-long piece by ripping the piece in two at a 45-degree angle. The top cleat is glued under the back of the top frame as shown. The bottom cleat has mounting holes drilled in it and attaches to the house. Sand the entire project with 150-grit sandpaper, and apply the finish of your choice.

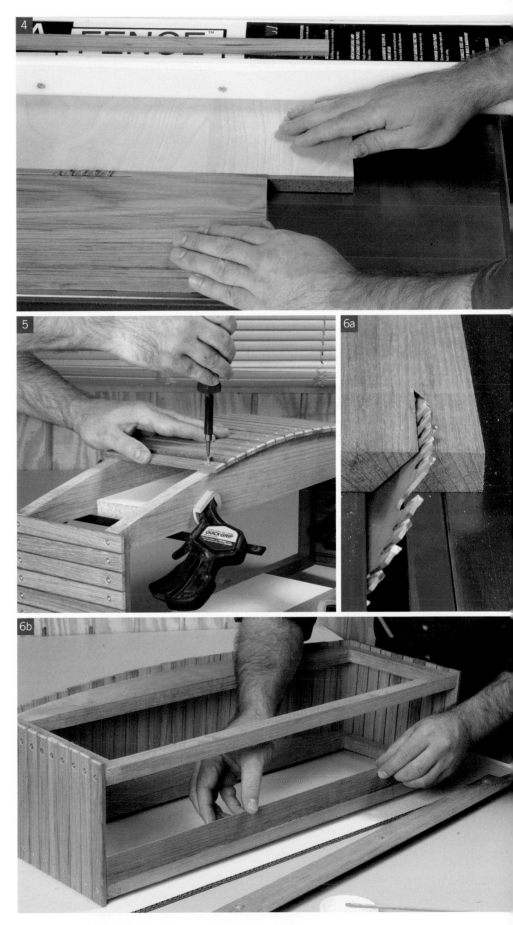

materials, tools, and techniques

DID YOU FIND your perfect table or must-have chair? Whichever project in the preceding section attracts you most, you'll want your own version to last. Here, the basics of materials, tools, and techniques will help you craft an enduring, functional piece. ❧ *Because outdoor furniture has to weather the elements, the materials involved are vitally important. Naturally, you want the piece you craft so carefully to last for years, and to sustain your own satisfaction in a job well done. So you need to carefully select not only the wood, but also the fasteners, adhesives, and finishes.* ❧ *Just as important, the way you build a project will have a huge impact on how well it survives both Mother Nature and day-to-day use. Whatever your skill level, we will guide you through all the techniques you will need to create something worthy of your time.*

choosing wood

It's smart to spend some time understanding the choices of wood available for outdoor projects. Basically, what you're after are woods that are naturally resistant to moisture and the rot and decay it causes. Woods are classified into two broad groups: softwoods and hardwoods. Both types can be excellent choices for outdoor projects—depending on what you're making, how much you want to spend, aesthetics, and of course, the purpose of the piece.

SOFTWOODS

WESTERN RED CEDAR is one of the most decay-resistant species in America; it's completely non-resinous, so it offers no "food" for decay. It grows along the coastal ranges of western Canada and the United States, from Alaska south through British Columbia, Washington, and Oregon, and east to Idaho and Montana. Western red cedar's tendency to split makes it perfect for shingles and shakes; when exposed, it weathers to an attractive silver gray. Because it isn't a very strong wood, though, it's a poor choice for furniture that's under stress, such as chairs.

CALIFORNIA REDWOOD, probably the most familiar wood for outdoor furniture, grows very fast and is decay- and insect-resistant. No wonder it's the most commercially valuable softwood in America. It grows along the coastal northwest of the United States. Like cedar, redwood is soft and has relatively low strength, so it should not be used for furniture under high stress. (Incidentally, this is the reason the classic redwood picnic table is so clunky: The wood is so soft you need thick pieces to stand up to wear.)

PRESSURE-TREATED PINE (typically Southern yellow pine) is the most common wood in outdoor construction because it's the least expensive. Although this lumber holds up well against the elements, it's typically very wet inside, even after sitting in a lumberyard for a while. This excess moisture wreaks havoc on your tools and is best reserved for simple "cut-and-bolt-together" projects such as children's play sets.

The standard pine you find at home centers is fine for many outdoor projects, as long as you protect the wood with a quality primer and topcoat (see page 126 for more on this). Pine is relatively inexpensive, readily available, and easy to work with.

HARDWOODS

The top three hardwoods for outdoor projects are mahogany, teak, and white oak. Each of these offers superb strength and durability characteristics, and all are excellent choices for high-stress projects such as chairs, benches, and rockers. As you might suspect, costs can be steep, but you get what you pay for.

CHARACTERISTICS OF OUTDOOR WOODS

WOOD	STRENGTH	EASE OF USE	DECAY RESISTANCE	COST
Cedar	Poor	Easy	Excellent	$
Mahogany	Good	Moderate	Good	$$
Pine	Fair	Easy	Poor	$
Redwood	Poor	Easy	Excellent	$$$
Teak	Excellent	Difficult	Excellent	$$$$
Treated pine	Fair	Moderate	Good	$
White oak	Excellent	Moderate	Excellent	$$

Sustainable-Growth Alternatives

In addition to the familiar outdoor woods already described, there are a number of lesser-known woods that offer similar properties, but often at less cost. And, they are usually harvested from sustainable-growth forests.

 BOCOTE (also known as cordia or ziricote) comes from the West Indies and tropical America and is an excellent substitute for teak. It's almost as dense and hard, but it's nowhere near as abrasive to tools—or as expensive. The heartwood is rich, golden brown with a pinkish tint.

 JARRAH is harvested in Australia and is so immune to Mother Nature that it's used for shipbuilding and marine structures such as dock pilings and bridges. The heartwood of jarrah is brownish red and is often marked with short, brown radial flecks on the end grain and boat-shaped flecks on the flat-sawn surfaces.

 IROKO comes from equatorial Africa and is sometimes referred to as African teak. It's widely used for boat-building. The heartwood of iroko is light brown to rich golden-orange brown. Like teak, iroko blunts cutting tools. Wear a dust mask when working with this—iroko sawdust can cause respiratory problems.

 CHECHEM (pronounced chey-CHEM) is another excellent substitute for teak. Chechem grows in the Dominican Republic, Cuba, Jamaica, Guatemala, Belize, and Mexico. The heartwood of chechem is amber to dark brown, often with a range of colors and contrasting streaks.

To find a source for sustainable woods in your area, visit the Certified Forest Products Council (CFPC) website at *www.certifiedwood.org*. CFPC is an independent, non-profit organization whose mission is to "Conserve, protect and restore the world's forests by promoting responsible forest products buying practices throughout North America."

AFRICAN MAHOGANY grows in West, Central, and East Africa. It's highly prized in furniture construction because it's a dream to work with—it carves well, holds details, and does not damage your tools. (Its ability to be carved explains why mahogany was the wood of choice for classic Chippendale furniture.) Mahogany is regularly used in boat-building for trim, where it's referred to as "brightwork"—a result of the numerous coats of high gloss varnish applied to it.

TEAK is the ultimate outdoor wood. It's strong, hard, and very dense. It's resistant to all insects, fungus, and marine borers; termites won't touch it. And it resists rot and moisture. Teak is distinctively oily to the touch; oil in the grain makes it very durable. What's the catch? First, it's the most expensive of the outdoor woods (only the wealthy use it on their yachts). And second, it's extremely abrasive. Teak severely blunts cutting tool edges; even carbide-tipped blades will dull while working this tough wood.

WHITE OAK is very resistant to wear, insects, and fungi, and it's also practically waterproof. The sap-conducting pores of American white oak are naturally plugged, yielding its water-repellency. It's used for "wet" or tight casks and is especially prized for aging and storing wine, bourbon, and whiskey. This natural aversion to water makes white oak a great choice for your outdoor projects.

In general, a softwood board is graded as a whole piece, whereas a hardwood board is graded on its usable content. The actual grade for a piece of softwood lumber is calculated with a complex formula that considers the type, size, closeness, frequency, and location of all characteristics and imperfections with the piece (see the chart on page 109). For the most part, the clearer the board, the higher the grade and the more it will cost. C&BTR (a grade meaning letter C and better) is a good choice for outdoor projects since each board may contain only two small, sound knots. Common boards contain knots, and most are unsuitable for outdoor projects unless the knots are well sealed and the project is painted.

BUYING SOFTWOOD LUMBER

Most softwood lumber is used in construction and is cut to standard sizes. This lets architects and builders around the world all use the same "building blocks" when designing or building a structure. The length of a softwood board is given in actual dimensions, and the width and thickness are given in "nominal" dimensions; actual dimensions are somewhat less. This means that a 10-foot 2 × 4 is really 10 feet long, but not 2 inches by 4 inches—it's actually 1½ inches by 3½ inches. Nominal dimensions are based on rough-cut, green lumber; actual dimensions describe boards after they've been dried and surfaced on all four sides (see the chart at right).

Although softwood dimensions are standardized, softwood grades are not. As softwood is often used for structures, its grading system must take into account strength, stiffness, and other mechanical properties. The problem is, no two woods have identical characteristics, and so every softwood species has its own set of grading guidelines. Almost a dozen organizations publish grading guidelines. Because each grading organization has different names and specifications for the softwood grades, it's difficult to compare them.

NOMINAL VERSUS ACTUAL SOFTWOOD BOARD SIZES

ITEM	NOMINAL THICKNESS	DRESSED THICKNESS	NOMINAL WIDTH	DRESSED WIDTH
Boards	1"	¾"	2"	1½"
	1¼"	1"	4"	3½"
	1½"	1¼"	6"	5½"
			8"	7½"
			10"	9¼"
			12"	11¼"
Dimension	2"	1½"	2"	1½"
	2½"	2"	4"	3½"
	3"	2½"	6"	5½"
	3½"	3"	8"	7½"
	4"	3½"	10"	9¼"
	4½"	4"	12"	11¼"

BUYING HARDWOOD LUMBER

Hardwood logs are typically cut "for grade" to obtain the best yield of usable wood. Because too much good wood would be lost trying to convert each board to a uniform dimension (as in softwood lumber), hardwood lumber is sold in random widths and lengths, pretty much as it comes off the saw. Hardwood lumber is sold by the board foot, a volume measurement that indicates thickness and width as well as length. One board foot equals 144 square inches.

To determine the number of board feet in a given board, measure the width and length in inches. Then multiply the width times the length times the thickness and divide by 144. For example: Say a board is 1 inch thick, 10 feet long, and 6 inches wide. The calculation would be $1" \times 120" \times 6" = 720"$. Dividing by 144 gives 5 board feet.

Boards thicker than 1 inch can get confusing because of the "quarter" designation system that is still used today, but is based on the cutting capabilities of early sawmills. These older machines could cut only in $\frac{1}{4}$-inch increments. Because of this, lumber was sold in "quarters"—three-quarters ($\frac{3}{4}$ inch), four-quarters ($\frac{4}{4}$ or 1 inch), six-quarters ($\frac{6}{4}$ or $1\frac{1}{2}$ inches), and so on. It's important to note that this measurement is for rough, *unsurfaced* lumber. But most hardwood today is sold *surfaced* (see the chart below).

The foundation of the hardwood grading system is the cutting unit method. According to the National Hardwood Lumber Association (NHLA), a cutting unit is "a portion of a board or plank obtained from crosscutting or ripping or by both. Diagonal cuttings are not permitted."

Basically, the grade of a board depends on the total area of clear cuttings the board will yield in relation to its total square footage or surface measure. Each grade specifies how much clear wood the board will yield: roughly 83 percent for FAS (firsts and seconds) and select, about 67 percent for number 1 common, and 50 percent for number 2 common. (See the chart on page 109.) For the most part, you'll typically find only one grade—FAS—at lumberyards. Select and common boards are usually found only at mills, as they don't offer the higher profit potential of FAS.

"QUARTER" DESIGNATORS FOR HARDWOOD

QUARTER DESIGNATOR	ROUGH THICKNESS (inches)	(mm.)	SURFACED THICKNESS (inches)	(mm.)
4/4	1	25.4	$\frac{13}{16}$	20.6
5/4	$1\frac{1}{4}$	31.8	$1\frac{1}{16}$	27.0
6/4	$1\frac{1}{2}$	38.1	$1\frac{5}{16}$	33.3
8/4	2	50.8	$1\frac{3}{4}$	44.4
10/4	$2\frac{1}{2}$	63.5	$2\frac{1}{4}$	57.2
12/4	3	76.2	$2\frac{3}{4}$	68.9
14/4	$3\frac{1}{2}$	88.9	$3\frac{1}{4}$	82.6
16/4	4	101.6	$3\frac{3}{4}$	95.2

SOFTWOOD GRADES FOR BOARDS

CLASSIFICATION	GRADE	APPEARANCE
Select	B&BTR	Many pieces are absolutely clear and free from knots; only minor defects and small blemishes are permitted
	C select	Small defects and blemishes allowed; recommended for all finishing uses where fine appearance is essential
	D select	Defects and blemishes are more pronounced; used when finishing needs are less exacting
Finish	Superior	Only minor defects and blemishes allowed
	Prime	Similar to superior but with more defects and blemishes allowed
	E	Pieces where crosscutting or ripping will produce superior or prime grades
Common	#1 common	The ultimate in fine appearance in a knotty material; all knots must be small and sound
	#2 common	Contains larger, coarser defects and blemishes; often used for knotty pine paneling

HARDWOOD GRADES FOR BOARDS

GRADE	FACE GRADED	MINIMUM YIELD	COST	CHARACTERISTICS
FAS (Firsts and Seconds)	Worst	$83\frac{1}{3}$% of board is guaranteed usable	$$$$	Boards must be at least 6 inches wide and 8 feet long; best used when long, clear boards are needed
Select	Best	$83\frac{1}{3}$% of board is guaranteed usable	$$$	Similar to FAS, but the best side must grade FAS and the worst side #1 Common; good for parts where only one side will show
#1 Common	Worst	$66\frac{2}{3}$% of board is guaranteed usable	$$	Boards and cuttings are shorter and narrower than FAS, and the cuttings are the same quality as FAS, just smaller; this grade is great for smaller parts
#2 Common	Worst	50% of board is guaranteed usable	$	Small boards and cuttings require extensive work to extract usable wood from a board; common in furniture manufacturing because it's so cheap

COMPOSITES

Although composite decking and decking products have been around for years, it took a while for them to start showing up in local lumber yards and home centers across the country. Composite deck boards are made from recycled plastic and ground-up wood fibers, with the intent of offering the best of both materials.

Since part of the composition is wood fibers, composite decking will weather over time; since the wood fibers are small, there is no risk of splinters. The benefit of adding plastic is that the deck boards are much more stable: no warp or splitting. Trex, Choice-

Dek, Tek-Dek, and Nexwood are all popular choices. The main difference among these products is the type of materials used to produce them. Although most are solid, some (like TimberTech) are extruded to form a structural plank.

Another choice that has recently become available to consumers is 100 percent recycled plastic lumber. Although most diehard woodworkers shun this material, it offers some real advantages over wood and even composites. First, since there is no wood involved, the product is truly dimensionally stable—it won't expand and contract due to changes in relative humidity like wood does and some composites can. Second, it won't crack, split, or fade. It's environmentally friendly and comes in a wide variety of sizes and colors (white, teak, redwood, cedar, and gray, just to name a few).

Surprisingly, plastic lumber costs more than pressure-treated lumber, but you'll save money in the long run since there is no long-term maintenance—no chipping paint, no repainting, no yearly coats of varnish. For sources of plastic lumber, check out the National Recycling Coalition's Buy Recycled Business Alliance at *www.brba.nrc-recycle.org.*

It's important to note that both composites and plastic lumber should never be used for structural purposes. But as long as they're supported, they hold up extremely well over time. Another plus: When you're done constructing your project, you're done—there's no finish to apply (see pages 62–67 for a set of planters made from plastic lumber).

Plastic Lumber

The finish-free aspect of a project made from plastic lumber is nice, but what most woodworkers will love is that it's unbelievably easy to work with. That's because there's no grain at all to worry about. Cutting into this stuff is like cutting into a stick of butter: It's the same through and through. There is no grain to splinter or tear out, no warp to worry about, no wood movement problems of any kind.

fasteners

If you're not using joinery (see pages 120–123) to hold parts together for an outdoor project, you'll need to use some kind of a mechanical fastener. Screws are the best choice for most jobs; others call for specialty fasteners.

SCREWS

There are five types of outdoor screws (left to right in the photo below): stainless steel, vinyl-coated (see sidebar at right), bronze, galvanized, and brass. The most commonly available and least expensive of these are galvanized screws. These are basically steel screws covered with a galvanized coating to prevent rust. Although they're inexpensive and easy to find, the coatings can chip off when the screw is driven into a board.

Bronze screws stand up extremely well to the elements. Their dark color makes bronze an excellent choice for a Western cedar or redwood project, since the screws will blend right in as the piece ages.

Brass screws, although good looking, tend to strip and/or break easily as the metal is so soft. If you do use brass screws, always drill pilot holes.

Stainless steel screws are another good-looking choice for outdoor projects. They're virtually impervious to the elements, and their glossy finish works well with high-end pieces. They are, however, quite expensive.

Regardless of the material you choose for a screw, whenever possible select square drive heads versus slotted or Phillips head screws. The unique square recess in the screws heads (and matching screwdriver or driver bit) greatly reduces the tendency of a standard bit to "spin" while driving in a screw. This is particularly important with outdoor furniture, where screws have a tendency to freeze in place over time, making removal difficult.

SPECIALTY FASTENERS

Carriage bolts (also known as carriage screws) are large bolts that are partially threaded and feature a smooth, rounded head. Beneath the round head is a square shank that bites into the wood as a nut on the end of the bolt is tightened. These are particularly useful when access to one side of the bolt is limited and you won't be able to reach the head with a wrench.

Lag bolts (also called lag screws) are basically heavy-duty screws that are driven in with a wrench. Lag bolts offer a convenient way to secure parts together, but do not offer the strength of a carriage or machine bolt that runs completely through the parts and "clamps" them together via a washer and nut.

Some outdoor projects (such as a folding table) will require moving parts. Hinges should be solid brass, brass-plated, or stainless steel to stand up to the elements. Piano hinges offer a lot of support while being unobtrusive. Eye bolts and eye screws are used to support projects such as porch swings; these are commonly available in a galvanized finish.

Fasteners to Avoid

A relative newcomer to the fastener market, vinyl-coated deck screws are touted as weather-resistant. The screws are coated with a thin layer of vinyl that seals the metal. The problem is that when you drive the screw through a piece of wood, the coating rubs off.

Nails are another type of fastener to avoid. Without threads, they don't grip the wood, and over time normal expansion and contraction of the wood will cause the nail to "pop."

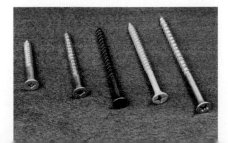

adhesives

For projects that don't rely on mechanical fasteners to hold them together, adhesives and tight-fitting joints are the alternative. The type of adhesive you choose will depend primarily on the materials you're bonding together (see the chart below). Generally, adhesives that need mixing are messy but are also the strongest. One-part adhesives are convenient but not as strong. So, a snack table will do just fine with an adhesive that won't stand up to the stress of a chair.

CROSS-LINKED PVA (POLYVINYL ACETATE) is an exterior-rated yellow glue and the most commonly used outdoor adhesive. Like regular yellow glue, it sets up quickly (about 15 minutes), and clamps need to be applied for about one hour.

EPOXY is an excellent choice for an outdoor adhesive. This glue has a couple of advantages over others: It fills gaps well and doesn't require clamps. It comes in quick- and longer-set versions; go with the longer-set since assembly can be stressful enough without having to play "beat the clock." Epoxy is usually mixed in a 1:1 ratio of hardener and resin and is the adhesive of choice for oily woods like teak.

RESORCINOL was for many years considered the best all-around outdoor adhesive. It is virtually impervious to water even when submerged. Like epoxy, it's a two-part system that's messy to work with. Its other drawback is its red color, which makes glue lines stand out. If you're painting the project, this isn't a concern. But if you're using a clear topcoat, choose another adhesive.

POLYURETHANE is a newcomer that is as versatile as epoxy but doesn't require mixing. It does have its disadvantages, though. If it gets on your skin, it's difficult to remove—make sure to wear rubber gloves. And, although a bead of polyurethane will expand two to three times its size to fill gaps, the foamy substance has no strength.

CONSTRUCTION ADHESIVE AND SILICONE are two other adhesives that are useful for outdoor projects. Construction adhesive fills gaps, sets up without clamps, and is surprisingly strong. Although most folks don't consider silicone an adhesive, it offers excellent adhesion properties combined with flexibility. Both of these come in cartridges that fit standard caulk guns.

CHARACTERISTICS OF OUTDOOR ADHESIVES

TYPE OF GLUE	PROPERTIES	DURABILITY	COST
Construction adhesive	Weatherproof varieties are available; needs no clamping	Fair	$
Cross-linked PVA	No mixing required; sets up moderately fast and is fair at gap filling	Good	$
Epoxy	Requires mixing and sets quickly; fills gaps well, but is messy	Excellent	$$$
Polyurethane	No mixing, very messy, works well with wet wood such as pressure-treated lumber	Good	$$
Resorcinol	Must be mixed, dries reddish in color, and requires long clamping time	Excellent	$$$
Silicone	Stays flexible in all weather conditions; difficult to clean up	Excellent	$$

finishes

A project finish is more than a finishing touch: It beautifies the wood but also protects it against the elements. Not all wood needs protection, though. Cedar, redwood, teak, and white oak can be left unfinished and will all turn a weathered gray over time. Less-decay-resistant woods need protection from moisture, the sun, and dirt.

CLEAR TOPCOATS include polyurethanes and spar varnishes. Each of these penetrates into the wood and allows the natural beauty to show through. Spar varnish has more "solids" to create a thicker, more durable coat. Select one that has a UV inhibitor, and expect to reapply the finish every two or three years, whichever type you choose.

STAINS let you alter the appearance of the wood while protecting it at the same time. You can either tint the wood with semi-transparent stains, which allow you to still see the wood's grain, or use an opaque stain for a complete cover-up. Both kinds require regular maintenance in the form of annual re-coats.

PENETRATING OILS, such as Danish oil or teak oil, soak into the wood and create an excellent barrier against moisture and dirt. These finishes do not build up, so they're not a good choice if you want a glossy finish. Like stains, penetrating oils need to be reapplied annually.

PAINT is a good choice when you want to cover up wood (such as pine or pressure-treated pine), or you want to add color to your furniture. Always start with an oil-based primer before applying the top-coat of paint.

Solvent- vs. Water-Based Finishes

One of the decisions you'll have to make regarding a finish is choosing between a solvent- and a water-based finish. Water-based finishes (both stains and topcoats) offer the advantage of easy cleanup. On the downside, all water-based finishes "raise" the grain of wood and must be sanded lightly between coats to knock off the raised fibers. Water-based clear topcoats take some getting used to: They look like diluted glue as you apply them. The good news is that they dry to a clear finish.

Although solvent-based finishes are messy to clean up, they impart color to the wood, which helps bring out the grain, and they dry to a tough, durable surface. You will rarely find boatbuilders using a water-based topcoat. They have been using solvent-based spar varnishes for decades, and for a good reason—the varnishes last.

PROPERTIES OF OUTDOOR FINISHES

TYPE	SURFACE SHEEN	DRYING TIME	DURABILITY	COST
Paint	Flat to gloss	Latex: 1–2 hrs. Oil: 3–6 hrs.	Latex: durable Oil: very durable	$
Penetrating oil	Flat to semi-gloss	1st coat: 2–4 hrs. 2nd coat: 24 hrs.	Does not protect against abrasion, but helps keep piece clean	$$
Polyurethane	Satin to gloss	24 hrs. between coats	Durable	$$
Spar varnish	Satin to gloss	24 hrs. between coats	Very durable	$$$
Stain	Flat to semi-gloss	4–6 hrs.	Does not protect against abrasion, but resists fading	$$

woodworking tools and techniques

In the pages that follow, we've tweaked some traditional wood-working techniques to make them accessible to the average homeowner. You'll find lots of time-saving tips and tricks to get professional-looking results. Maybe you don't (yet) know the difference between a bar clamp and a backsaw. Or you've never heard of a half-lap joint. The point to knowing terms like these, and applying them to your projects, is that they help you create good, sturdy pieces that stand up to use and time.

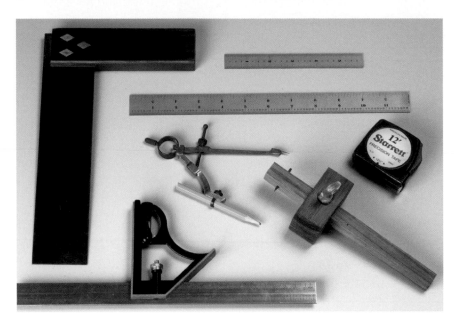

MEASURING AND LAYOUT TOOLS

Of all the many techniques you'll use to build a piece of outdoor furniture, the two that will affect everything else you do—from cutting and drilling to final assembly—are measuring and lay out. That's why the tools you select to measure and lay out parts are so important. You'll find the following tools helpful (shown clockwise from the top left in the photo): try square, 6-inch metal rule, 12-inch metal rule, 12-foot tape measure, marking gauge, combination square, and compass.

A try square is used to lay out boards for joinery and to check edges to make sure they're truly square. In use, the wood stock is pressed up against the edge of a board and the blade is used to check for square or a pencil is drawn along its edge to mark a line.

Six-inch and 12-inch metal rules are extremely handy for laying out joinery and checking machine setups, such as the height of a bit or blade. Look for metal rules where the graduations are etched into the surface instead of printed on, as printed graduations wear off over time.

Probably the most used measuring tool in the shop is a steel tape measure. For the projects in this book, a 12-foot tape measure is all you'll need.

A marking gauge is useful for marking parallel lines with precision, such as when laying out joinery. The standard marking gauge has four parts: a beam, a fence, a thumbscrew, and a marking pin. To use a marking gauge, loosen the thumbscrew and slide the fence along the beam the desired distance from the pin. Tighten the thumbscrew and place the fence against the edge of the workpiece and angle it so the pin tilts away from the direction you'll slide it. Now slide the fence along the edge of the workpiece with even pressure, and the pin will mark a perfectly parallel line.

Some folks prefer a combination square to a try square because it combines the functions of a metal rule, a try square, and a depth gauge. A combination square has a metal rule with a groove in it that accepts a metal head. The head has both a 90-degree and a 45-degree face. Loosening and tightening the knurled nut on the head lets you slide the head back and forth on the rule.

A compass is useful for laying out curves and arcs. The most common type (shown above left) is a wing compass that has legs joined at the top with a spring; the legs are forced open or closed by turning a knurled knob that attaches to a threaded post that spans the legs. One leg has a steel point; the other holds a pencil.

HAND TOOLS

In addition to layout and measuring tools, there are a number of other hand tools that you'll find useful in building outdoor furniture. Shown clockwise from the top left

in the top photo: jack plane, 4-foot bar clamp, C-clamp, 4-in-1 screwdriver, sanding block, 4-in-1 file/rasp, backsaw, hammer, coping saw, rubber-faced mallet, set of chisels, hand saw, and 16-inch bar clamp. A sharp jack plane will make quick work of leveling surfaces and cleaning up rough cuts. Bar clamps, pipe clamps (not shown), and C-clamps are all designed to draw parts together during assembly. The backsaw, coping saw, and hand saw are used for cutting joinery, curves, and pieces to length or width, respectively. The hammer, mallet, and screwdriver are essential for assembly. A set of sharp chisels, along with a file/rasp and a sanding block, is indispensable for trimming parts and fine-tuning joints.

POWER TOOLS

Although you could build all the furniture in this book with hand tools, portable and stationary power tools will save you a lot of time and effort. With corded and cordless portable power tools, you take the tools to the work. With stationary tools, you bring the work to the tool.

Shown clockwise from the top left in the bottom photo: circular saw, router, random-orbit sander, cordless driver/drill, and saber saw. Circular saws are great for cutting boards to width and length. A router with a set of edge-profiling bits can quickly cut joinery and decorative edges on parts. A random-orbit sander will rapidly smooth parts, and a cordless driver/drill is useful both for drilling holes and for driving screws during assembly. The saber saw excels at cutting curves.

Stationary tools (not shown) such as the table saw, band saw, and power miter box make woodworking even easier, but they don't fit into everyone's budget or workspace. If you can't afford these (or they won't fit in your workshop), try to find a woodworking club in your area. Occasionally, you'll find one that has a group shop where you can rent tools by the hour or day.

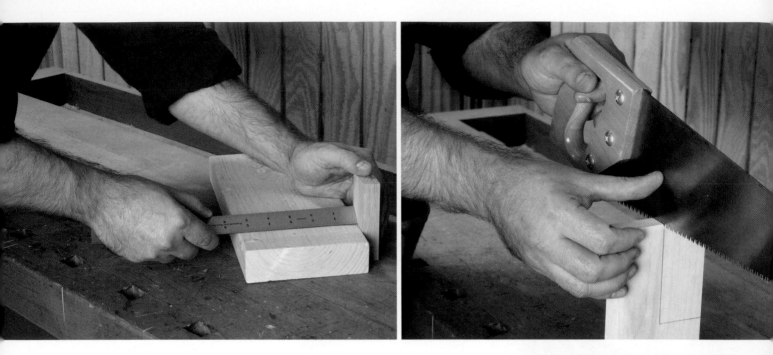

MEASURING AND MARKING

Precision in measuring and marking can be achieved with accurate tools, patience, and proper technique. One of the simplest things you can do to add precision to your layout work is to use a mechanical pencil instead of a standard pencil. With a mechanical pencil, the replaceable lead creates a crisp, even line; a standard pencil produces a line of varying thickness as the pencil wears. This may not seem like much, but it can introduce significant errors over a long workpiece, such as when laying out joinery.

When using a metal rule to measure in from an edge, try butting a scrap of wood against the edge of the workpiece to serve as a stop (above left). This positions the end of the rule absolutely flush with the edge of the workpiece, resulting in very accurate measurements.

MAKING STRAIGHT CUTS

Whether you're using a hand saw or a power saw, to make a straight cut you need to start it straight. You can always correct an errant cut, but you'll be better off starting straight in the first place.

To make a straight cut with a hand saw, first use a combination or try square to mark the square cut line. Then clamp the workpiece in a vise or to a sawhorse. Next, use your thumb to guide the saw blade to the waste side of the cut (above right). Try to keep the saw and your hand, elbow, and shoulder all aligned. Draw the saw back a few inches to start the cut and then continue sawing, keeping the blade pressed constantly against your thumb as a guide.

Another trick to making an accurate, straight cut is to use a scrap of wood to guide the blade as you cut. To do this, clamp a known-square scrap block to the workpiece so one edge is flush with the marked cut line (right).

Then, start the saw by taking a few short backward strokes and continue sawing, keeping the saw blade pressed firmly against the guide block.

Straight cuts with power saws are quite easy with a couple of simple aids: a speed square and

a rip fence. The speed square is used to guide a circular saw for making cross cuts—that is, across or against the grain to cut a board to width. The rip fence is used with a circular saw to rip a board to width along its length.

A speed square has a lip on one edge that hooks onto the edge of the workpiece. The edge that's perpendicular to the lipped edge of the square then serves as a guide for the saw. All you do to make a cut is slide the square over so it positions the saw on your marked cut line (above left). Hold the speed square firmly in place (you may want to clamp it to the workpiece) and make the cut by sliding the saw base along the edge of the square.

To rip accurately with a circular saw, attach a rip fence to the saw base. Rip fences are standard with some saws or can be purchased as an accessory. Adjust the fence so that the saw blade aligns with your marked cut line. Then,

keeping the fence pressed firmly against the edge of the workpiece, make the cut by sliding the saw along the length of the board (above right).

MAKING CURVED CUTS

Curved cuts are more challenging because you can't use a guide. Instead, steer the cut by hand. You can make curved cuts with a coping saw, a saber saw, or a band

saw. The secret to accurate cuts with any of these tools is patience. Take your time making the cut, and keep your marked line exposed by frequently stopping and blowing away sawdust. Try to keep your cut about $\frac{1}{16}$ inch from the marked line on the waste side (below). This makes it easier to sand or file the curve to its final shape without having to remove excess wood.

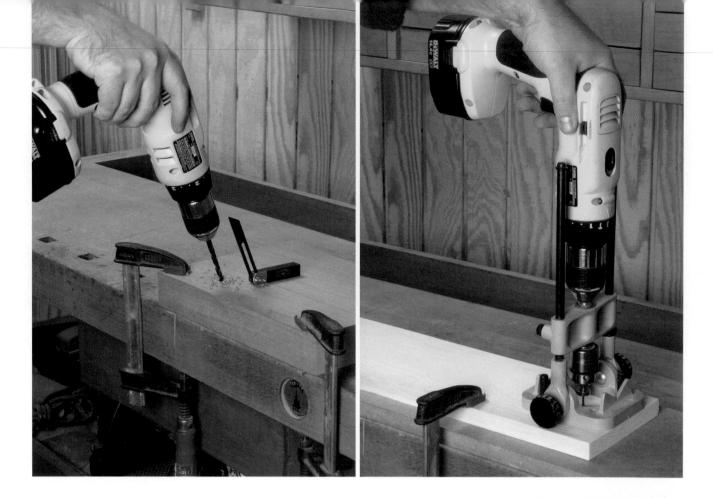

DRILLING PRECISE HOLES

Virtually every outdoor project you build will need holes for dowels, fasteners, etc. A drill press delivers the ultimate in precision, by keeping the bit perpendicular to the workpiece as it bores. But not everyone has a drill press, and quite often the holes must be drilled during assembly, where a drill press isn't practical. Here's where portable drills come into play. The only problem with a portable drill is that its precision is only as good as your eye-hand coordination.

Fortunately, there are a number of aids you can use to add precision. One such aid is a bubble level. These small, inexpensive, self-adhesive levels can be attached to the top and back of a drill to show when the drill is plumb and level. For angled holes, another trick is to use a sliding bevel gauge

as a sight aid. Just adjust the gauge to match the desired angle and place it on the workpiece. Align the drill bit with the gauge and drill (above left).

Another nifty aid is a drill accessory called an adjustable drill guide (often referred to by the brand name Portalign). This device basically turns your portable drill into a small drill press. You insert the shaft of the guide into your drill chuck and insert a drill bit in the guide's chuck, and you're ready to drill precise holes (above right). The large base provides a stable platform and easily adjusts between 45 and 90 degrees.

assembly techniques

Assembling a project can be both frustrating and rewarding. It's great to watch your project take shape—as long as everything goes together well. That's why advance planning and preparation are essential for successful assembly. This means taking a dry run without glue to make sure everything fits. This also forces you to have all your clamps on hand and makes sure that not only do you have enough, but also that they are long enough and can exert sufficient clamping pressure. Remember that if you have to use a clamp to force a

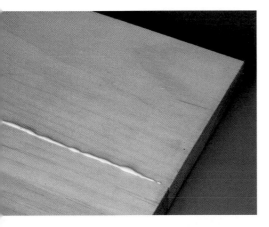

part to fit, it doesn't fit. Take the time to fine-tune the fit and check it again.

When everything fits, you're ready for glue. Have on hand plenty of glue, glue brushes, clean rags for removing spills—and your clamps, including clamp pads (see the sidebar at right). Apply the glue to one section at a time— typically an assembly such as the side of a bench or chair. Brush on enough glue to coat the surfaces

to be mated, but don't get carried away here. What you're after is a continuous bead of glue showing at the joint once the clamps have been applied (left). Less glue than this indicates a starved joint, which can result in a weak assembly.

Like glue, the amount of pressure applied to clamps is often overdone. All you need is to close up the joint so that the parts fit snugly together. If the joint does not fit, do not compensate with excessive pressure, fix the problem. Even with care, though, sometimes assemblies will be out of square, or "racked." You can check for this by measuring diagonally across the corners—the measurements should be the same. If they're not, apply a clamp diagonally across the assembly and adjust the clamp pressure until they match (above).

Clamp Pads

Using a clamp without a pad is about the same as banging parts together with a hammer—both will leave marks. Pads for clamps can be as simple as scraps of wood inserted between the clamp face and the workpiece. Another solution is to dip the clamp faces in liquid plastic to create a cushion. Or you can buy rubber pads that slip over the clamp heads to prevent marring. Regardless of what type you choose, use them religiously to prevent frustrating marks that can be a real hassle to remove.

COMPARING BASIC JOINTS

Butt joint

The butt joint is the weakest of all wood joints and is made by simply butting two pieces of wood together. Without fasteners, this joint offers very little strength. But when glue and screws are applied, the joint can provide adequate strength, and it's quick and easy. One way to make this joint stronger is to use metal framing connectors such as joist hangers to support and tie the pieces together (see page 49 for an example).

Miter joint

A miter joint joins two pieces of wood together at a corner so that no end grain is exposed. Because they are end grain to end grain, the joint is weak unless fortified with dowels, biscuits, or splines (see page 46 for an example).

Half-lap joint

A lap joint is formed whenever two parts are lapped over one another. In furniture construction, both ends of the pieces are typically notched so the surfaces end up flush with one another—this joint is technically called a half-lap and does an excellent job of resisting lateral movement.

Dado joint

A dado is a U-shaped cross-grain cut on the face of a piece of wood that's sized to accept another part. Dadoes are cut across the width of a board; the width of the cut matches the thickness of the other part. Care must be taken to use sharp cutters to prevent tear-out while cutting cross grain.

Groove joint

The cousin of the dado is the groove—a U-shaped cut that's made *with* the grain instead of across it. The ledge that's created by cutting a groove or dado supports the other part, making both an excellent way to lock one part into another.

Rabbet joint

A rabbet is an L-shaped notch that's cut into the end or edge of a part. This notch is sized to accept another part. This offers a better gluing surface than the butt joint and also serves to lock the pieces together during assembly. But like the butt joint, this joint needs to be reinforced with fasteners to have strength.

Mortise-and-tenon joint

Without a doubt, the mortise-and-tenon is one of the strongest joints in furniture construction. That's why it's used almost exclusively for joining together high-stress or high-load parts, such as the sides of a chair or bench. The mortise-and-tenon has two parts: A hole (usually square) called a mortise is made in one part, and a tenon is cut on the end of the mating part. Tenons are cut by removing wood on all four sides at the end of the part, creating shoulders. The tenon fits into the mortise and can be glued in place or held via dowels, fasteners, or even a wedge (see page 16 for an example).

BASIC JOINERY

There are seven common joints, shown in the chart at left, used to construct all of the furniture in this book. Each can be cut by hand or with power tools.

BUTT JOINTS should always be reinforced with glue and fasteners. Screws are your best bet, and metal framing connectors work well to connect parts that won't be seen—such as the bench frame of the planter bench shown on page 44. But even with screws and glue, a butt joint isn't that strong. The reason is that the screws are driven into end grain, which has no holding power. One trick to strengthen a butt joint is to use a dowel to provide the necessary holding power (above).

Here's how. Start by drilling a stopped hole (a stopped hole doesn't go all the way through the part) about 1 inch or so in from the end of the part you're going to screw into. Drill the hole on the underside so it won't show, and size it to match a dowel, preferably at least ¾ inch in diameter. Then cut a length of dowel to fit in the hole and glue it in place, making sure that the grain of the dowel is perpendicular to the screw. Now as you screw the parts together the screw will "bite" into the dowel and pull the joint tight.

HALF-LAP JOINTS are easily cut by hand with a back-saw. Begin by carefully laying out the cut lines on the pieces to be joined. Then clamp the part in a vise or on a sawhorse and start the cut using one of the techniques described on page 116. As you cut, take care to keep the saw straight and level (top right). Half-laps are also easy to cut on the table saw using a dado set or on a table-mounted router using a straight bit.

DADO, GROOVE, AND RABBET JOINTS

can all be cut by hand, but are much easier to make with power tools. A portable circular saw with a rip fence or edge guide can make these cuts by taking a series of passes until the desired width is reached. An even easier alternative is to cut them on the table saw using a dado set— a set of blades that are stacked together to make a wide cut in a single pass.

Dadoes—across-the-grain cuts—are made using the miter gauge of the table saw along with the rip fence (bottom right). Position the rip fence so the dado aligns with the cut lines on your workpiece. Adjust the blade height and make a test cut in a scrap of

wood. Butt the scrap against the rip fence and push it slowly into the blade; adjust the blade height or rip fence as necessary and then make your cuts in the actual pieces. Rabbets are cut in much the same manner, except an auxiliary fence (just a strip of wood) must be clamped to the rip fence to prevent the dado set from damaging the fence (see page 66 for an example).

Dadoes, grooves, and rabbets can also be cut with a portable router or a table-mounted router. Whenever possible, you'll be better off making partial passes instead of one full-width pass. Not only is this easier on your bits and router, but it also creates a perfectly centered groove when you flip the piece end-for-end after the first cut (above). It takes some trial and error to position the router fence properly, but it's well worth the effort.

MORTISE-AND-TENON JOINTS

should be fit together by cutting the mortise first, then cutting the tenon to fit. It's much easier to resize a tenon than it is to recut a mortise. Although there are stand-alone mortising machines, they're expensive. A low-cost alternative is to make a mortising jig for your router (see the sidebar below).

To use the mortising jig, first mark the ends of the mortise on the workpiece and clamp it firmly to a bench so it extends out past the edge. Then place the router and jig on the workpiece and pivot the unit until both bolts butt up against the sides of the workpiece (below). Position the router bit (either a straight bit or a spiral mill bit) at the top mark. Turn on the router and lower the bit into the workpiece about ¼ inch. Keeping the bolts pressed firmly against the sides of the workpiece, slowly pull the router forward until you reach the other mark. Turn off the router, raise the bit, and return to the start. Continue making passes until the full mortise depth is reached.

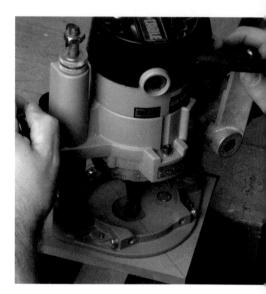

The tenon is simpler to cut. Install a dado set in the table saw, and position the rip fence the desired distance away from the blade to define the length of the tenon. Raise the blade and make a test cut using the miter gauge. Adjust the blade height or the rip fence as necessary. Note: You'll need to either square up the corners of the mortise with a chisel or round over the corners of the tenon with a file or rasp. Which method you choose is a matter of preference—either will create a strong joint.

Router Mortising Jig

One of the simplest ways to cut mortises is to make a mortising jig for your router. The jig replaces your existing router base and houses a pair of cut-off bolts that guide the router during its cut. The beauty of this jig is that it's self-centering. That is, as long as you keep the bolts pressed up against the sides of the workpiece during a cut, the mortise will be routed in the exact center of the workpiece.

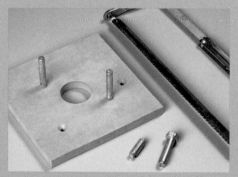

To make the jig, cut a piece of ½-inch plexiglass, MDF (medium-density fiberboard), or plywood to match your original base. Use your original base to mark the hole for the bit and the holes for the mounting screws, and drill appropriate-sized holes. Then mark one diagonal and measure 1⅝ inches out from the center in each direction and drill a pair of ⅜-inch holes. You will need to counterbore these so the heads of the bolts will be flush with the surface. All that's left is to cut the threads off two 3¼-inch-long, ⅜-inch-diameter stove bolts with a hacksaw. File the ends smooth, and glue the bolts in the counterbored holes with epoxy. Once it's set, attach the jig to your router and you're ready to go.

Mortises come two ways: stopped and through. A stopped mortise does not go all the way through the workpiece; a through mortise does. Both can be cut using a router jig, but there's a sneaky way to cut a through mortise: Don't cut a mortise. Instead, cut a pair of matching dadoes on the inside faces of two pieces and glue these together (right) to create a "no-mortise" mortise. For this technique to work, the parts need to be of identical thickness, and care must be taken during glue-up. One way to ensure that the halves align is to insert a scrap tenon key into the mortise during assembly. The only problem with this is it's easy to glue the key in place; to prevent this, apply a couple coats of polyurethane to the key and let it dry before using it.

FAUX MORTISES

When you need to cut many mortises, you can save yourself a lot of time and effort by cutting faux mortises. Instead of cutting the mortises individually, you can "mass-produce" them on the table saw in strip form, then glue them into a matching groove in the part to be mortised.

Here's how it works. Start by cutting a groove in the edge of the part to be mortised. Say, for example, you want to create a series of ¾-inch-long, ¾-inch-wide mortises that are ⅜ inch deep—you'd cut a ¾-inch-wide, ⅝-inch-deep groove. The next step is to cut or plane stock to fit the groove you just cut. In this case, it would be ¾ inch thick and the same length as the groove.

Now comes the fun part: Cutting the "mortises," which are really just notches at this point. They become mortises once they're glued into the groove; the walls of the groove form the sides of the mortises. To accurately cut a series of evenly spaced notches, you'll need a jig that attaches to the miter gauge of your table saw. This jig is just a scrap of wood with a cut-off screw in one face to serve as an index pin. Make a mark on the face of the jig 3 to 4 inches in from the end and up about ⅜ inch. Drill a pilot hole to

accept a #10 × 1½-inch wood-screw and drive the screw into the hole until just the shank is exposed. Then cut off the head, leaving just the shank, and file the end smooth.

Install a dado set in the table saw to cut a full-width mortise. Attach the jig to the miter gauge so the pin is to the *right* of the blade and is positioned to leave the desired amount between the notches. Make a test cut and adjust as necessary. To cut mortises in your strip, start by butting the strip up against the pin and making a pass (below left). Then lift the strip up and place the notch over the pin; slide the strip to the right until the edge of the notch you just cut butts up against the pin, and make another cut. Continue like this, lifting and butting the notch edge against the pin until you've cut all the notches.

All that's left is to cut the strip to width so it will fit flush with the edge of the grooved strip—in this case, ⅝ inch wide to match the depth of the groove you cut. Glue the strip into the groove so the "mortises" are centered from end to end (below right). With outdoor furniture, silicone caulk and epoxy are good adhesive choices.

advanced construction tips

If you look closely at the design of many of the projects in this book, you'll notice a common theme—slats. Virtually all of the horizontal surfaces and many of the vertical ones are made up of individual, narrow slats. The reason for using these instead of wider, solid pieces is that the gaps between the slats allow water to drain off and provide room for the wood to expand and contract as the humidity changes. This is especially important for outdoor furniture, which undergoes wild humidity swings from blistering sun to downpours.

The only challenge to working with slats is making them identical in shape, something that's especially important if the parts are curved. You could cut each piece and then try to sand them to match, but odds are they'll end up noticeably different. There is, however, a technique used in the furniture construction industry called pattern routing that can be adapted to the home shop.

This entails making a pattern and using this to duplicate the parts. The key to this technique is a special router bit called a patternmaker's bit (above left). It's basically a straight bit with a bearing mounted below the bit;

few pieces, but if you're duplicating a lot of parts, it's worth the time to make a jig to hold the parts as they're routed. The jig not only holds the parts in place, but the edge also serves as the template. Fast-action toggle clamps (below) are a great way to secure the parts to the jig while still letting you quickly remove and change the parts.

ENLARGING PATTERNS

Many of the projects here require making a pattern for a curved or angled part. Enlarging a pattern can be as easy as connecting the dots. Start by taping together enough graph paper to draw the

Spacer Blocks

You'll often need to drill a series of holes or make a number of repetitive cuts with precision. One of the best ways to ensure accuracy is to use spacer blocks to position the workpiece instead of relying on the layout lines. Spacer blocks are nothing more than a group of scraps all cut to match the desired spacing between the holes or cuts. In use, you simply drill a hole (or make a cut), insert a spacer block between the workpiece and a fence, and drill; continue to insert blocks and drill (or cut) as needed.

the bearing is the same diameter as the bit. By attaching a template to a workpiece, you can guide the bearing along the edge of the template and the straight bit will trim the workpiece to the identical shape of the template.

There are a couple of ways to attach a template to a workpiece. One is to affix it with double-sided tape. This works fine for a

pattern (1 inch grids can be found at most art stores, or you can lay out your own with some patience). Next, transfer the points where the pattern crosses a grid line from the pattern you're enlarging to your paper pattern. Then for straight lines, connect the dots with a ruler. When lines curve, connect the dots freehand, or use French curves or a flexible edge.

applying finishes

Regardless of whether you're applying stain, paint, or a clear topcoat, the secret to success is preparation. You can't get a smooth, flat finish if the underlying surface is rough. Creating a smooth surface entails both sanding and careful vacuuming. Sanding is best done with aluminum oxide open-coat sandpaper beginning with 120-grit and ending with 180-grit—always *with* the grain. Anytime you sand, you'll end up with a layer of sawdust and sanding grit on the wood that needs to be removed prior to finishing. Not only can this residue mar a finish, but it can also stop the finish from adhering to the wood. To prevent this, vacuum the project after the dust has settled and use a soft-bristle brush adapter to prevent dings and dents.

STAINS

Stains are a wonderful way to change the color of a project while still allowing the wood grain to show through. You may want to stain a piece so that it matches others in a set, or to subtly change its shade or add a burst of color. In addition to the classic colors for outdoor furniture (redwood, cedar, etc.), there are many colorful options available.

Staining is basically a two-step operation: Brush on the stain, and then wipe it off. The exception is if you're using a water-based stain. Manufacturers of these products

recommend you "condition" the wood prior to staining by brushing on a conditioner, letting it dry, and then sanding lightly to remove the raised grain that will result from using a water-based product.

Make sure to stir the stain thoroughly—most of the pigment will settle at the bottom—and stir

it periodically as you use it. Brush the stain on in small sections. Allow it to rest the recommended time, then wipe off with a clean, soft cloth, first against the grain and then with the grain (above).

Choosing a Brush

There are three main types of brushes to choose from: natural, foam, and synthetic. Which brush you choose depends on the finish you're applying. Natural-bristle brushes are a good choice for oil-based stains and clear topcoats, since they excel at absorbing and holding a finish. Unlike natural bristles, which soften and become uncontrollable in water, synthetic bristles keep their shape and so are best used with water-based stains and finishes. Foam brushes are becoming increasingly popular for all finishes (including paint) because they don't leave brush marks and are inexpensive enough to throw away when the job is done.

NATURAL

FOAM

SYNTHETIC

PAINT

Painting outdoor furniture requires the same sanding and vacuuming as for any finish. But there are other important steps required before the first coat of paint is applied if your project is made out of softwood and has any knots—even tightly closed ones. Knots in softwood are very resinous and can ooze out or "bleed" over time. You can't completely prevent this, but you can slow it down considerably by brushing on one or two thin coats of shellac to seal the knots.

PRIMING The next step is to apply a quality primer/sealer to the entire project. Don't cut corners—it's important to prime all surfaces, including the undersides of parts. Following the manufacturer's

directions, apply a coat of primer/sealer to the project with a foam or natural-bristle brush; oil-based primers hold up best over time (above).

SANDING BETWEEN COATS Most primers need to be sanded once they're dry to create a smooth foundation for the paint. Your

best bet here is to use 220- or 240-grit wet/dry sandpaper. Sand all surfaces lightly (below left) and then vacuum the project thoroughly.

PAINTING Now that the project has been primed, sanded, and vacuumed, you can apply the actual paint. Again, oil-based paints hold up best. Work on the underside of the project first, then flip it over and do the top; this lets you catch any drips or runs that will be highly visible. Brush on a thin coat (below right), taking care to leave as few brush marks as possible. Once the paint is dry, sand lightly again, vacuum, and brush on one or more additional coats until you've achieved the desired finish.

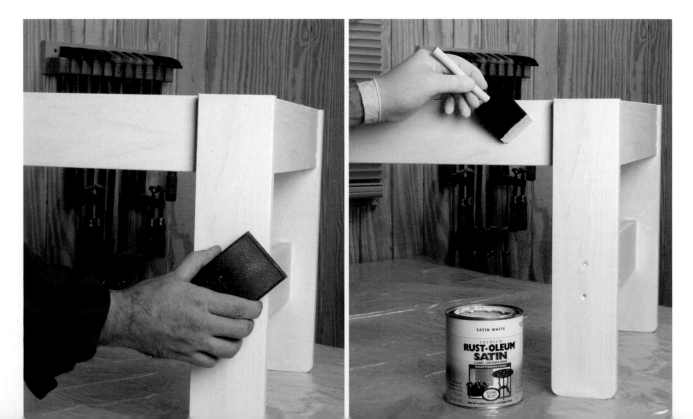

CLEAR TOPCOATS

A clear topcoat may seem like an easy finish to apply: You just brush it on and you're done, right? Not so, especially if you're after a smooth, flat finish.

As a general rule of thumb, the glossier the finish, the more effort is required to get a flawless finish.

That's because the shiny surface of the glossier finishes (right) shows even the tiniest imperfections. One way around this is to select a semi-gloss, satin, or flat finish.

No matter which topcoat you choose, it's best to apply multiple thin coats instead of a single heavy coat. When you apply thinner coats, you should sand the project lightly between coats with 220- or 240-grit wet/dry sandpaper and then vacuum. This eliminates bumps and ridges and creates a smoother surface. With a thinner coat, there's also less chance of finish building up in nooks and crannies, resulting in a sag or run.

It's also a good idea to wait a couple of minutes after the finish has been brushed on and inspect it carefully with a light held at a low angle; you're looking for sags and runs. Remove any excess finish from your brush by wiping it on a clean cloth, and then go back and brush out any runs or sags that you've found.

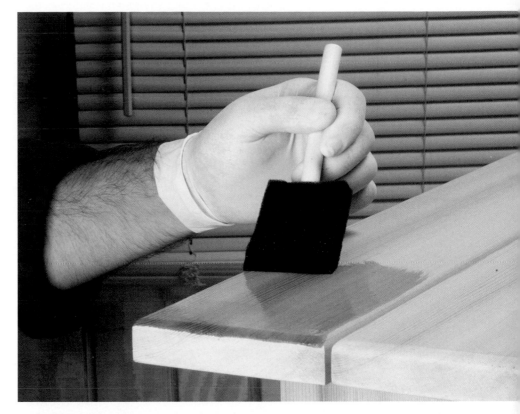

Finishing "Oily" Woods

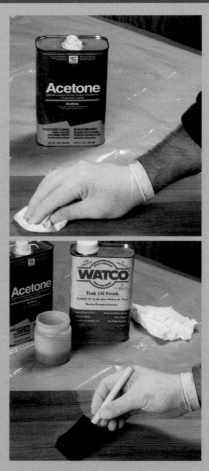

Hardwoods that contain natural oils, such as teak, have a well-deserved reputation for being tough to finish. The problem with these woods is that their natural oils create a barrier that a wiped- or brushed-on finish can not penetrate—so the finish won't adhere to the wood. The solution is to temporarily remove the barrier and then quickly get the finish on. You can remove the surface oil by wiping the wood down with acetone or lacquer thinner.

As soon as the acetone evaporates, be prepared to apply the finish. Topcoats that build up a finish (such as polyurethane and varnish) can still have problems adhering to the wood; you'll be better off applying two or three coats of penetrating teak oil—just make sure to follow the manufacturer's application instructions.

index

Page numbers in **boldface** refer to photographs.